What Faith Has Taught Me, Inspiration for All and Quotes About God.
By The Prophet of Life

What Faith Has Taught Me

Spiritual Insights From The Prophet of Life

The Faith Trilogy

3 Faith Filled Books by The Prophet of Life

It is our pleasure to bring you this very special paperback
edition of three faith filled books by The Prophet of Life.
Each book offers different insights into faith.
The first book, What Faith Has Taught Me gives readers personal insights
into faith. It goes from the faith that existed even in horrors
of The Prophet of Life's youth (in Where Was God?) through insights
into faith that he came upon recently (How Everything is Connected).
The second book, Inspiration for All is full of positive, uplifting stories
of inspiration. Many of the stories are family oriented (A Tribute to Mothers,
Fatherhood). Others are kid oriented (Teenage Mysteries of Life Solved).
Still others are topical (The True Meaning of Failure). We are sure you will
enjoy all of these stories.
The third book, Quotes about God is full of interesting and profound quotes

about God attributed to The Prophet of Life. Within its pages you will find
quotes that inspire you, sustain your faith and that show you new ways of looking
at God. Our staff favorite is: "People often wonder why God allows hunger, poverty and war
in our world. Perhaps God wonders why we allow it."

Cover Photo: A cloud formation Jesus in his robes presenting The Sacred Heart as seen by
The Prophet of Life near The Sanctuary in 2016.

Inspiration for All
Selected Stories of Inspiration
By The Prophet of Life & Mark Wilkins

A Matter of Perspective
Inspirational Quotes

Quotes about God

A Whole lot of Quotes about God

Preface

This book came together as a culmination of many different factors. The Prophet of Life has over 20 different books attributed to him. His books range from faith filled to topical subjects. Quotes attributed to him are used throughout the world by institutions of higher learning, institutes of medicine and scholars. We wanted to bring together three of his faith filled books to create a faith trilogy in one paperback edition. We chose his most popular faith book What Faith Has Taught Me, his book Quotes about God and a very special collection of his inspirational writings, stories, quotes and essays which we call Inspiration for All. If you are a person of faith, we are sure that this special trilogy for years to come.

What follows is the introduction to What Faith Has Taught Mc.

I am just an ordinary person who has been privileged to have a life filled with miracles and revelations. There are many times when I had nothing except faith but faith was all I needed to sustain me. My faith and my God have taught me many life lessons. My faith taught me to work towards a better day instead of being childishly upset when I didn't get it immediately. My Faith has taught me to forgive because forgiveness frees me to move on to something better. My faith has taught me that all life is precious and so I respect all life, even life forms that others take for granted.

My intention in writing this book is to share some of the things my faith has taught me and the spiritual insights I have gained because of my faith. Some of the insights are presented as life lessons I have experienced and am now passing on and others are presented as a series of questions which I call the What If Conversations. The insights contained in this volume are constructed from life lessons and have shaped my world view which is spiritual in its foundations but touches upon global and cultural issues as well. It is my sincere hope that you will find some things of value.

What My Faith Means To Me

Every morning when I wake up, it is faith that empowers me to get out of bed. It is faith that propels me through the day. It is faith that guides me, bobbing and weaving around numerous perils that are in my path, be they perils of my environment or perils from the destructive nuances of my own personality. My faith shows me the limitless possibilities of each day. It is faith that delivers me back home at the end of each day. It is faith that shows me what The Lord wants me to see that day and faith that teaches me the lessons that give me the insights that I have been credited with.

I cannot even imagine what the world is like for someone with no faith. It must be very scary indeed to live in a world filled with so much cruelty, destruction and death and not believe that there is a purpose, to it all. It must be difficult to live the drudgery of each day like a zombie, one day blending into the next with no distinguishable difference between them. To live a life without hope that something better is coming.

For what is faith, except a perspective on life seen through the belief that there is a purpose, there is hope, there are miracles, there is something better coming, there is a loving God. I have witnessed so many miracles in my life that I know there is a loving God behind them. God's existence for me is unquestionable and undeniable. If Scientists declared that there was proof that God does not exist I would submit evidence to refute it. If the whole of humanity stopped believing in God and hope, I would stand like a lone candle, burning in the darkness to light the way with the light of truth. That is why, the symbol of my faith is a lone candle illuminating the darkness because all who are of faith, no matter which faith we hold, are like candles illuminating the darkness.

Once we are all joined together in the truth that we are all branches of the same tree, that tree will prosper. Once we understand that we may have differences but that we are all equal in God's eyes, we can end the destruction of religious war. Once we resolve with mutual respect, to work together to solve the problems we face as human beings and as a planet we can begin to actually solve them on a global scale.

My faith doesn't depend on miracles or wish fulfillment to sustain itself, although I have witnessed many miracles, they are not what sustains my faith they are merely confirmations of it. My faith has taught me that The Lord is not a fairy godfather who waves a wand and makes all your problems disappear but a teacher who gives you the tools to solve your own problems and shows you the way to do it. My faith tells me that The Lord communicates with everyone but that not everyone is listening. My faith doesn't tell me that "The Lord works in mysterious ways', but that The Lord works purposefully and that bad things will happen to all of us but that they only serve to teach a lesson that once learned, will open the way to something better.

My faith is true faith but I know that it is no better than anyone else's faith. It's just different. That knowledge allows me to build bridges with other people of faith even though their faith is different from mine because I always keep in mind that my faith is different, not better and so is theirs. My faith has no limitations. That is okay, because neither does God's love.

Where Was God?

I was always a rather sickly child. When I was about one and one half years old, I went into severe convulsions. I ended up in a coma for eight weeks. Where was God?

When I was two or three years old, I was afraid of the dark. I tried to tell my parents but my mother was too busy working trying to support our family and my father was too drunk to care. Where was God?

When for the first few years of my life, I watched helplessly as my parent's marriage disintegrated before my eyes, ending in bitter divorce before my fourth birthday. Where was God?

When I was sent to live with strangers, far away from both my parents; where was God?

When I spend years of my childhood living under the control of these strangers and was physically, mentally, emotionally and sexually abused, where was god?

When I was six and one half years old and ran away from one of the homes I was sent to, intent on committing suicide by walking up a hill to a cliff and jumping off, where was God?

When at nine years old, I was back with my mother and we moved into a different apartment and the first night, as I lay in bed, a ghost kept scratching my back and calling my name and I was too afraid to move, or yell, or cry for help, where was God?

During all of the trials and tribulations I suffered from infancy through adulthood, where was God?

There are times when we feel that God has abandoned us but in reality, that is just our perception. God never abandons anyone.

When I was one and a half years old and went into convulsions, I actually died. A tall, thin, bearded man in his early thirties, came into my house. He said he was there to heal me. He told the paramedics that he saw the ambulance parked in the driveway and he came in to help. The paramedics told him he was too late, I was dead. Yet, the man insisted on trying to help. The paramedics, assuming that he was a doctor, let him while they worked on my grandmother. The man found a way to get my heart to start beating again. He showed the astonished paramedics that He had revived me. Then he left, never to be seen or heard from again. God was there.

After I was transported to the hospital by the paramedics, I laid in a coma, packed in ice for eight weeks. Although they had run batteries of tests on me, the doctors could not find the cause of my convulsions. I maintained a high fever despite the ice packed all around to cool me down. At the end of the eight weeks, my condition had declined to the point that doctors told my mother make funeral arrangements.

My mother went in the hallway, outside of the hospital room and began weeping. As she wept, a bald headed, Asian man in a monks robe approached her. He came over to her and asked her why she was crying. Assuming he was a visiting Doctor, she told him about my ordeal and my impending death. He asked her what tests they had run on me. She listed the many tests run upon my tiny body. He listened and then asked if the doctors had checked my ears. My mother wasn't sure. The man told her to tell the doctors to check my ears. I had two infected ears. Once they realized this, the doctors were able to cure the problem and I came out of the coma. When my mother asked the name of the Asian Doctor who had helped her, so she could thank him. The doctors replied that that hospital didn't have any Asian doctors on staff and that they didn't have any visiting doctors either. God was there.

When I was an infant, afraid of the dark, I would pray for help. Somehow, I knew about God even though I had never gone to any religious services. When I prayed, I would see, a tiny light appear in the corner of the ceiling. It wasn't bright enough to light the room, but it was bright enough to let me know that I was safe and that although I was surrounded by darkness, light was still present. God was there.

When I helplessly witnessed the disintegration of my parent's marriage and was placed in the homes of strangers who repeatedly abused me, I learned lessons and developed compassion for those who suffered similarly. When I became a responsible adult, I helped them and served as an example that it was possible to come out of that hell and still lead a normal life. God was there.

When I was nine and the Ghost scratched my back and called my name all night long I was truly frightened. The next day, when I asked my landlord if anyone had died in my room, he told me his mother did. The haunting and scratching continued but didn't bother me because I realized that what I thought was a dangerous presence was merely a mother, trying to rub a child's back to help it go to sleep. God was there.

Through all of my trials and tribulations from infancy through adulthood, God was there, with lessons to teach me and the knowledge gained from them to comfort me in future times of affliction. So the next time you are going through a trail or tribulation, try to find God in it because God is there.

How Would You Describe Your Faith?

If you were to describe your faith in just one sentence, what would that sentence be? Not the religion you belong to but your individual faith in God. Everyone, despite their faith, has an individual relationship with God. That relationship constitutes your true faith.

There are some who practice their religion fervently but don't bother with their one to one relationship with God. Others never go to a temple or church or shrine but are in constant contact with God, praying or meditating or just relating. Some see God in a building, others see God everywhere. So how would you describe your faith?

One of the What If Conversations series…

What if the purpose of life is to learn what it has to teach us?

What if the obstacles and setbacks we experience are only tests meant to make us stronger?

What if the failures we experience are only meant to teach us what not to do in the future?

What if we are meant to learn, not only from the mistakes we make but also from the mistakes of others?

What if every life experience, no matter how brief or pointless it seems on the surface contains a deeper meaning in the lessons it can yield from the knowledge gained and lessons taught both to the spirit experiencing that life and to the rest of humanity and the universe?

Knowing this, would pain and suffering be purposeless or meaningless?

If the purpose of life is to learn what it has to teach us…

What have you learned?

How the Way You Act Affects Your Environment

If you take a skipping stone and skip it across a lake, the water ripples. Just as the stone affects the water in the lake, you affect the environment around you by the way you interact it. In fact, how you act creates the environment around you. Here are two examples of this from my life that happened to me recently.

The first one happened while I was standing in line at the grocery store, I observed a man leave his cart in the checkout line. He went to the next aisle to get something he forgot. A lady passed by him and walked over to the line the man had just left. Within seconds, seeing no one there the lady moved his cart away and jumped ahead of him in line. The man returned within fifteen seconds and by then, the woman had already put four things on the conveyer belt. The man asked the woman why she moved his cart and jumped in front of him. The woman replied that he wasn't there so he lost his place. The man and woman got into an argument. Other people in the market watched and as the argument escalated so did the tension in the air. Soon other people began arguing about who was right and who was wrong in the argument between the man and woman.

The second one happened later that same day, I was in line at a chain restaurant. I had a coupon sheet with several coupons and was asking if it was still good, as I believed that day was the last day before the coupons expired. There was a man behind me who had to wait a little longer because of my extended interaction with the cashier. After I gave the cashier the coupon I selected from the sheet I turned to the man who had been standing behind me and apologized for his delay. I offered my coupon sheet to him so he could also take advantage of a coupon if he found something he liked. He used a coupon on the sheet. Then he handed the sheet to the woman standing behind him in line and she also used a coupon on the sheet. They both became more animated and struck up and conversation with each other and with me.

My actions made both of those people smile and changed the environment from isolation to friendly. This is something anyone can do. Anyone can pass on a coupon sheet that is about to expire and offer it to their fellow customers without expecting anything in return. You might consider doing this some time and see if it changes the environment around you.

How Everything is Connected

One day, while I was watering my backyard, The Lord taught me the following lesson. As I was watering the grass, I noticed part of the tree root popping out above the grass about 20 feet from the tree. It was then that The Lord came to me and said:

"If you wish to water the tree you must not only water it at the base of the tree but you should also water where it's roots crop up all over the yard." Said The Lord. "Stop and look." He continued, "at all of the places where the tree root crops up in your yard."

I did so. I found about a dozen places.

"If you don't water all of those places", The Lord continued "The tree will wither and die in the places where you do not water. Not watering the entire tree, in all of the places where its root crops up hurts the tree. In this way, the tree is connected to your yard and your yard to the tree." The Lord pointed out.

"This tree in your yard can also represent the tree of life on this planet." The Lord continued, "All life on this planet is connected. If you neglect one part of the life on this planet, be it an individual or an entire species of plant or animal, you harm all life on this planet because all of life on this planet is connected just as the roots of this tree are connected."

With that, the lesson ended. I had always known about the connection of all life on our planet but The Lord put the connection together in such a simple, yet profound way that for the first time, I really understood the concept. I am merely relating this interaction here so that you might understand it too.

Are You Where You Want To Be In Your Life?

It's a good practice to review your life periodically to see where you are in regards to where you want to be. We all have dreams. We all have goals. Reviewing your life periodically can help you clarify whether or not you are achieving them. First, take a look at the seven major areas that make up your life and assess where or not you are satisfied with them. The seven areas are food, shelter, family life, social life, close friendships, love life, working life and growth.

You should ask yourself questions about each of the areas of your life. Are your food and shelter needs taken care of? Do you have good family relations? Do you have a social network that can support you? Do you have any really close friends who you can confide in? How is your love life? How is your work life? Are you in a career you love or just in a job? Are you growing or just staying the same?

Where you are in each of these areas in reference to your happiness, usually depends on how close you are to goals you had made previously. People who are usually happy are either satisfied with their progress towards the goals they have set or they have no goals. People who are unhappy with any particular areas of dissatisfied with their life overall usually are not satisfied with their progress in achieving their goals.

When we are children, we often have no real responsibilities. We don't have to earn money to buy food or pay the rent. Because of this, when we are children, we can dream big because there are no obstacles to stop us. We imagine the life we want to have when we become adults. As we grow, the responsibilities pile up. We need to get good grades in school. We want to make enough money to buy something we desire. We get married and have to raise a family. The accompanying stresses also pile on. All of them grind us down little by little until we either have to alter our original dream of what our life would be like or defer the date we expect to achieve our goal.

In reality, where you are in life is where you actually want to be. This is because you have, all through the process made choices that affect your progress towards achieving your goal. You have made choices that help you towards reaching your goal and you have made choices which have impeded you from reaching your goal. In some instances, the choices you made that impeded you from reaching your goal were choices you couldn't help. In some situations the choice which impeded you was the ONLY choice you could have made. They may not have been technically your fault but you did make the choice and have to live with its consequences. It may not seem fair but life happens and the choices you make determine where you are in life.

If, after your life review, you find you need to improve in a couple of areas, begin to plan, step by step, how you will improve. What work needs to be done? How much effort needs to be applied? What time, finances or education needs to be changed to allow you to put the time and effort to achieve growth in the area you want to improve? Finally, if all else fails, give yourself a reality check. If you keep on working towards a goal and never make sufficient progress, then perhaps the goal is unrealistic. It may not be impossible to achieve it but given the time, effort and education you have, or have to devote to it, it may be unrealistic.

We all have goals. We all have dreams. We don't all achieve them. Those that do achieve their goals often plan work and progress incrementally towards them. They put the appropriate amount of time and effort into them. They make sacrifices. They make the choices that support achieving the goal. A Periodic Life Review can help put your progress in focus and by doing so, empower you to achieve your goals.

Giving to Get

Give to get is a big buzzword right now. Some corporations are using it to show that they are socially responsible. To show that they are giving back to the global community. Others use it as a way to describe providing their customers with more than they might otherwise expect. Both, in their own way are noble ideals.

What does give to get mean to the average person? Many are walking down the road of life believing that they have everything figured out. Some know about the law of attraction or Karma or the biblical verse about reaping what you sow. Then, something really bad happens to them and they begin to doubt the things they once believed to be truth.

The concept of Give to get is beyond corporate idealism. It is beyond platitudes that people carry with them but do not fully understand. Give to get is a concept that has power and a spiritual vibration that, when used correctly and with the proper intent, spirit, understanding, reason and action connects with the ebb and flow of the universe.

Giving to get is more than trying to realize a reward in this lifetime or paying a karmic debt forward. It creates an asset with rewards that are never ending. Giving to get done often enough in the right spirit evolves into giving for the sake of giving. This is where the true meaning of the concept becomes clear. This is where one may transcend the drudgery of everyday life and become one with the ebb and flow of the universe really kicks in.

Being one with the ebb and flow of the universe yields knowledge in lessons learned from mistakes made, realizes that failure leads to success finds hope for every distress and an answer for every question. It allows you to realize the purpose of your life and to live life purposefully. It reminds you that each of us has a social responsibility. And that each of us are a valuable member of the global community. It allows you to let the light that is within you illuminate humanity. That is the true meaning of Give to get.

The Difference between A Servant of God and Someone Working for A Reward

The difference between a servant of God and someone working for an eternal reward is that a servant of God serves God because God has shown them the work to be done and they do it. They do it because they know it needs to be done. They know that doing the work is part of their life's mission and they accept the action of doing it as a joyful duty. There is no reward expected other than the accomplishment that is felt when a task is completed. The work itself is enough.

Someone who claims to be a servant of God who is doing it for an eternal reward is not truly a servant of God. They are a servant to the concept that they will receive an eternal reward for their efforts. As such, they are no different than someone who volunteers at a charity event in hopes of running into a celebrity who can propel their career forward. If the celebrities don't show up, do they leave in the middle of the event? If the reward is taken off the table would they stop serving God?

Many who claim to serve God get more than an eternal reward. They attract people and along with people comes increased status and money. There is nothing wrong with increased status and money and talented people in all fields attract both. Using a perceived association with God to attract them is wrong. There are people who claim this from all five of the religions established by the five Original Great Religious Philosophies, Hinduism, Buddhism, Judaism, Christianity and Islam.

Look carefully and you will see them. Often, they are superstars and their personal aura clouds the meaning of their service. They may talk about their service a lot, they may even talk about God a lot but are they performing their service to God? Does their action outweigh their talk or does their talk outweigh their action?

Other times, they are not superstars. They are someone with more knowledge than you in a particular area. You hear about them and seek them out or they hear about you and they seek you out. Either way, they tell you they can help you. Then they offer to help you…for a price.

So next time someone who claims to be a servant of God or who claims to have an "In" with God crosses your path, look and see if they are truly a servant of God or merely a pretender. The reality is that there a many pretenders and few actual servants.

Gratitude: The Key to True Faith

What is the key to true faith? The answer to that question consists of one word: gratitude. Why gratitude? Because people who are truly faithful know and understand that life is a learning experience and God sends you what you need to learn the lessons your life has to teach you.

A Faithfully shallow person is like a sunshine patriot, they are happy to profess their faith and show gratitude in times of plenty, when everything is going their way. It takes a person of deep faith to profess their faith and show gratitude when life is hard everything seems to be going against them. Yet it is exactly people of deep faith that profit the most from times of challenge. This is because they are the ones who actually learn the lessons that the times of challenge are meant to teach them. They rarely repeat the mistakes that may have helped set them up for challenging times because they have learned the lessons.

People of shallow faith rarely learn the lessons that life is meant to teach them. They go through life looking only for the happy times and trying to forget the bad times. They never actually forget the bad times, however, they cling onto them, often unconsciously. They either repress them or try to mask them with addictions. Since they never learned the lessons that challenging times were meant to teach, they keep repeating the same mistakes and often face the same challenges over and over again.

Both people of shallow faith and people of deep faith pray. People of shallow faith pray for deliverance. People of deep faith pray for God's will to be done. People of deep faith are almost always okay with the outcome of times of challenge is. People of shallow faith are rarely okay with it. People of deep faith, of true faith, thank God for the experience and are grateful for what they have learned from it. People of shallow faith become upset with God for not answering their prayer and not delivering them from the experience. They don't see the lesson they should have learned because they are focused lack of avoidance of the experience instead of on the experience itself.

People of shallow faith depend on miracles and wish fulfillment to sustain their faith. People of deep faith, of true faith know that true faith does not depend on miracles or wish fulfillment to sustain itself. They are grateful for the experiences God sends to them, both good and bad because they know, that God only sends them experiences which can make them stronger from the lessons that they learn through them.

What if Perception Determines Reality?

Part of the What if Conversations Series

What if reality as we know it is nothing more than an agreed upon set of rules that we all follow?

What if the laws of physics were both true and not true? What if they were true for those who agree to follow them but can be superseded by those who don't agree?

This could explain the anomalies of a small group of people who have throughout our history seemed to defy physical laws. The Siddhas who can lift inches above the ground, the witch doctors, and sorcerers and warlocks who seem to be able to tap into an alternate consciousness to do things the rest of humanity knows are impossible.

What if reality was determined by one's perception and a change in perception could yield a change in one's reality?

Imagine the possibilities in human health, in conquering war and famine and pollution. This would mean that the first step in changing our world for the better is to change our collective consciousness. A change in our collective consciousness would lead to a change in our collective actions. We could, as one race, the human race, change our world. The world doesn't have to be polluted. Hunger doesn't have to be prevalent. Disease doesn't have to run rampant. War doesn't have to be declared.

It may be impossible to change the collective consciousness of all of humanity all at once. It is, however, possible to change the collective consciousness of humanity one person at a time. The Lord sent me these "What if" Conversations so that we may begin the conversations that will lead to changing the collective consciousness of humanity. If you have found this conversation, you have been chosen to be one of the people who begin the conversation. Whether or not you choose to participate is of course, up to you. Think about the issues raised here. Meditate upon them. Share and discuss them with your friends and colleagues. Begin the change.

An Example of How Your Perception Determines Your Reality

In a continuing effort to illustrate how your perception determines your reality I have written a story that can be seen from two different perspectives. Each perspective determines the reality of the person who holds it. One perspective can be seen as beneficial or good and the other can be seen as malevolent or evil.Each perspective could be from someone on the road next to the house who see two men entering via a side gate to the property. Read the story and then answer the question on the bottom. You must pick one of the two choices.

A House

The two men walked until they came to a huge gate,. "See, I told you today was a good day to come here." Said Pete

They entered through a smaller gate on the side. Tall bushes hid the house from the road. The pair strolled across the finely landscaped yard slowly. "Someone might see us." Bill worried aloud. "Nah", Said Pete, "No one can see us from the road." "So, the family is on vacation while the house is up for sale?" Said Bill.. "They sure are," Said Pete. "We've got this place to ourselves." He added.

They walked through the yard and up a hill. As they reached the downward slant of the hill the house came into view. "I never knew this place was so big". Said Bill. "No one does, that's the point, it's secluded to insure privacy." Pete responded.

As they got closer to the house they noticed that it had two French doors that opened onto the back yard and a door on the side of the garage. They entered the door on the side of the garage. There was nothing in the garage except three ten speed Italian racing bikes. At the end of the garage was a door which led to the house. Pete knew it would be unlocked because it usually is.

The door opened up into the living room. "I didn't know this place was so big." Said Bill. "It looks bigger since they added that 75 inch big screen television and surround sound." Said Pete. "And look at that fire place!" Bill pointed at a freshly installed, marble fireplace. Two solid Gold Grammy Awards stood on the mantle.

"Let's hear how the sound is on this baby." Said Pete as he turned on the television, changed it to internet mode and clicked on Pandora. He bumped his favorite tune which reverberated all over the house at an eardrum splitting volume. 'Turn that down!" shouted Bill. "Someone might hear it." He added. "Don't worry", said Pete. The whole house is soundproofed, you could set off a charge of dynamite and no one would hear it." He added.

Then they went off the spare bedroom. It was a state of the art recording studio filled with pricey outboard equipment. "Did this studio come with the place?" Bill askcd. "No, the owner had it built in but everything in it is removable so it can easily be cleaned." Pete said.

Then, the two men went into the Master bathroom. It had an attached bedroom with a sauna and spa bathtub. The bedroom itself had a huge walk in closet. Inside the closet was a fake wall. Pete knocked on it three times and a small room opened up. The room had a big safe in it. "Is this place sweet or what?" Asked Pete. "It's the sweetest." Responded Bill.

Are the two men a realtor and client or are they burglars?

The first perspective has the person passing on the road assuming that the two men are a realtor and a perspective client. The second perspective assumes that the two men are burglars. How the reader feels about the two men's race, dress, manner and even their own past experiences will determine which perspective they bring to the story. Which did you pick, realtor and client or burglar? Your perception of this story says a lot about your perception of life and the world in general.

A Blessing in Disguise

Have you ever had something bad happen to you, only to find out later that it was actually a blessing in disguise? Bad things happen to good people all the time but it while some hold on to the pain caused by bad things like it was a precious jewel, allowing that pain to hold them back from trying new experiences, others let it go and move forward with their lives.

It has been written that everything happens for a reason. It is true, everything does happen for a reason it's just that the person it is happening to often doesn't know what the reason was at the time things are happening to them. The reason usually only becomes clear in hindsight, after the incident has long passed and some perspective can be achieved.

So, what is the difference between the people who are devastated by the bad things that happen to them and those who seem to move beyond the trauma associated with the incident quickly? The people who move on quickly are often people in one of three categories: they are people of faith, spiritual people or people with a positive outlook.

People of faith often move beyond the bad things that happen to them because they have been taught through their religion that God watches over and protects them. They have a holy book, filled with stories and parables which illustrate this point. They have religious authorities that they can go to for guidance. They have a community of people who believe as they do, who they can count on for support. They move forward with the help of other people of faith as a member of a caring community.

Spiritual people believe in a higher power. They believe that higher power is ultimately good and that bad things are a part of life. They seek to learn the lesson that the bad thing was sent to teach them. They move forward because they know that the bad thing

That just happened to them happened for a reason. They may not know the reason just yet but knowing that it happened for a reason gives them the strength to move forward.

People with a positive outlook on life may not have religion. They may not even believe in higher power. They are strengthened by their honest belief that good things can come out of bad and that every cloud has a silver lining. They may also be bolstered by thoughts of how much worse the bad thing could have been and count themselves as fortunate that the bad thing wasn't a worse thing. They may also believe that something better is just around the corner. They move forward to get to that something better.

Are you in any of the three groups described above? Do you have a holy book, religious authorities and a community behind you? Do you believe that everything happens for a reason and search for the lesson in the event? Do you believe that every cloud has a silver lining? Or...are you a combination of two or more of these three types? If so, congratulations, you have evolved a coping strategy for the bad things that happen in life. If you do not fall into one of the three categories mentioned, what is your coping strategy? How has it been working for you? Do you let the bad things that happen to you hold you back or do you move forward beyond them? The next time something bad happens to you and trust me, something bad will happen to you sooner or later, remember the type of people that move beyond the bad things that happen to them and see what you can use that will work for you.

The Secret of Spiritual Growth

There are trials and tribulations in every life. There is sickness and disability. There are scars that heal slowly and scars that never heal completely. There is loneliness, loss and all manner of suffering. There is frustration and failure. There are dreams that are deferred and dreams that are never realized. It is not the defeats in life that defeat you but how you react to them. Those who learn the lessons that can be yielded from these experiences will minimize their effect and use them to become more than they were before they happened.

For in reality they are merely lessons. They may be hard lessons but they are merely lessons nonetheless. It is life's bitter moments that make its pleasant moments sweet. It is life's struggles that make the successes seem worthwhile. It is the difficulty of the uphill climb that gives the downhill coasting its full pleasure. It is the effort put into something that gives it its true value.

So let the trials and tribulations come; you can withstand them. Let sickness and disability nip at your body and slow you down; your spirit will propel you forward. Let the scars remind you, not of what you have lost but of what you have triumphed over. Let the loss and loneliness change what you value and let the suffering strengthen you. Let the frustration and failure teach you what not to do and make room for the wisdom that shows you what to do. Let them nag at you until you move beyond them into the next phase of your journey. Let the dreams deferred and never realized be replaced with dreams that can be realized.

How Believing Can Change The World

Belief is a powerful thing. Belief is what motivates humanity to do almost everything good and bad.

It is belief that has helped create everything ever invented. Belief helps determine perception and your perception determines your reality. What begins with one person's belief, can spread to others. In time, millions share the belief. This is called collective belief. For humanity to uniformly experience a more positive reality, we must first collectively believe that a better world is possible and then work towards it. Then our perception will change and along with it, our reality.

Being One with Nature

Today, while I was in my garden at the sanctuary, the place I live, I saw a few dozen hummingbird moths buzzing around and feeding on the nectar of flowers in one of the bushes there. Hummingbird moths are brightly colored insects about the size of a baby humming bird. They stay in flight and fly similarly to a helicopter just like hummingbirds do.

As I stood close to the bush, the moths buzzed all about me, feeding right in front of me as if I wasn't there. One was flying within inches of my nose. I leaned in towards him from behind my shallow breath creating a mist that gently passed over his back. He continued feeding as if I wasn't there.

The feeling was so magical, standing there among dozens of beautiful moths the size of a small hummingbird, enjoying the tranquility of the moment and participating with them in spirit. Things like this happen to me all the time in the sanctuary but I always marvel at them when they do. I also remember the mountain lion that befriended me there, but that story is for another time.

Part of the What if Conversations series…

What if there is more than one path to God?

What if all good people, no matter what their faith, can get into heaven?

What if all of the Prophets were really saying the same thing and when all of the things added on by their followers were stripped away the essence of all of these messages is:

Love God, Love yourself, Love each other, help one another and care for this planet and all who dwell here.

What if humanity spent less time trying to save souls and more time trying to save lives and improve the overall quality of life for everyone, no matter what religion, or nation or political ideology they were a part of?

What if all of the wars, and bombings and assassinations in the name of God, aren't really about God at all?

If any of these things are true, how would that truth change your perception of God?

How would it change your perception of humanity?

How would it change your perception of you relationship with God and your fellow human beings?

And finally… What if all of these things are true?

How Glorious Is Man!

How glorious is man. He walks upright in the day with the sun shining upon him. He enjoys and lives off the fruits of his land and his work and his mind. He is lulled to sleep beneath the stars with the rain falling gently upon him. How glorious is man.

How glorious is man. When the winds blow hard he withstands them. When the waters overflow he treads water. When the ground trembles or fires rage or hurricanes come he weathers life's storms. How glorious is man.

How Glorious is man. If he loses his home, he rebuilds it. If he loses his work he finds new work. If he loses loved ones he mourns them, remembers them but moves on with his life. How glorious is man.

How glorious is man. When his brothers mistreat him he stands up to them. When his brothers are ignorant he teaches them. When his brothers are hungry, he feeds them. How glorious is man.

How glorious is man. He learns to walk in the morning of his life, learns to run in the afternoon of his life, learns to relax in the twilight of his life and learns to fly at the end of his life. How glorious is man.

How glorious is man. He is born into a community of faith. He grows to develop his own personal faith and ends his life walking hand in hand with God. How glorious is man.

A Small Miracle with A Message

This morning, I awakened long before dawn, as I often do on weekdays before I work. I opened the refrigerator to get a cold bottle of water. To put in the blender for my protein shake breakfast. There was no cold bottle of water there. I searched the refrigerator thoroughly but still didn't find any cold bottles of water.

Then, I went to the pantry to get a warm bottle of water. I figured that warm water was better than no water at all. I got a warm bottle for myself and another for my wife. So that when she arose, two hours later, she could at least have a cold bottle of water for her protein shake breakfast.

I opened the refrigerator door and to my surprise, the appeared a cold bottle of water where none had been less than one minute before. At that precise moment, The Lord sent a message to me: "Those who provide for others shall in turn be provided for.

The Root Cause of Global Political Conflict

Battles raging between Israel & Palestine, Russia and Ukraine and in both Syria and Libya. Ebola and other viruses is spread from a few nations to other parts of the world. Many people are asking themselves one question, why?

Humanity has gone through more changes in the last 200 years than it had in the previous five thousand. This is because humanity has been passing from adolescence into adulthood. Our adulthood officially began on December 21, 2012. At that time a change occurred, but like most changes it merely was the beginning of a change, imperceptible to almost everyone. As time unfolds, however, the change shall become more apparent.

The narrow minded, selfish politics is the root cause of political strife across the globe. Leaders look at things solely from the point of view of their own nation, culture, religion or religious sect. People who look at things this way, advocating solely for their own group, often rise to power within that group. They are looked at as a voice or a champion for that group. It is that narrow mindedness that put them into a leadership position and, as we have seen with many leaders over time, once in power, few have the desire or courage to give that power up.

A new day is dawning in the global community. There is now, a strong global interdependence. No nation has the all of the natural resources it needs to completely sustain its people. In order to survive, all nations must trade goods with one another. The economy of individual nations depend on global economics. Because of this, conflicts are no longer regional because they have global consequences.

Those whose customs, views, religious practices and political actions go against the norms of the global community run the risk of being ostracized by the global community. Ostracization (a word which I have created but will in time, be in vogue as the practice is implemented across the globe) can include a host of travel, economic and trade sanctions that can devalue currencies and ruin economies. Repressive regimes have been falling all across the globe. This will continue. Although there will be despots who cling to power until the bitter end, the end will come in time. A new leadership shall arise which looks at things from a global perspective.

There is a popular saying: "Think globally, act locally". This has been the mantra of many for the last several decades. It is time for a new mantra: "Think Globally, act globally." Events will transpire which shall continue to drive home the point that we must live in harmony. That there must be mutual respect. That we must work cooperatively. The problems we are now facing and shall continue to face will be monumental in scale. So monumental that we will have to work cooperatively to survive. Take heart, nothing breeds harmony like adversity.

There are some who will think that this will fulfill a new world order, the rise of the antichrist, the end of the world or some other horrible consequence but they are wrong. In reality it is just part of our maturing process. It will, in the end fulfill the destiny of our race, the human race, for there is only one race and we are, despite what others may tell you, all one people under the blood.

As a soul, you as an individual go from one incarnation to another, one culture to another, one nation to another. You have experiences from one life to the next and, if you are wise, you learn lessons from them that last from one incarnation to the ones which follow. Humanity as a whole has a collective soul. The soul of humanity as a whole has a collective consciousness which learns collective lessons and has a collective destiny.

God only sends challenges to make us stronger and to prepare the way. It may not happen in our lifetime but in time, humanity will take its place, not as citizens of one global community but as citizens of a universal community. The lessons we shall learn during the times that shall follow will prepare us for this.

Towards Global Liberation

Every human being on this planet is entitled to basic human rights. Everyone should have the right to have healthful food to eat, clean water to drink, education, healthcare, sanitation and toileting facilities and to be treated with respect and dignity. The world has made tremendous progress towards these ends in the last century.

All across the globe, more people have access to healthful food and clean water. More children are being educated and world literacy rates are at an all time high. More health care is being offered to more people now than at any time in the world's history. More people have access to sanitation and toilet facilities. Human Rights are a reality in many of the world's nations.

The world is not, as we all well know, perfect. Across the globe a huge number of people go to bed hungry every night. Millions are without nearby access to clean drinking water. Millions are denied access to any education whatsoever for reasons of race, class or multiple births in one family. A billion people are without access to local healthcare.

Millions of people in the world are displaced from their homes due to war or racism. They have become refugees in other lands. Millions are still held in bondage as slaves. Wars continue to rage and civilian atrocities mount. Drug addiction rages in every corner of the globe. Crime continues and even death occurs at such an alarming rate that many are sensitized to it. People see it all on the news and ignore any atrocities that are not occurring in their own neighborhood.

An injury to one is an injury to all. If one person goes to bed hungry, all of humanity suffers. If one person is denied education our collective future remains ignorant. If one person is denied healthcare, disease spreads. If war rages in another part of the world it affects people in other parts of the world. If racism holds members of one race back no race is immune to its horrors. If one person is held in slavery, can any of us be truly free?

Now is the time to work collectively towards full world liberation. To create a world where all people enjoy basic human rights. To create a world where all people enjoy the equality of mutual respect and dignity. To create a world where no child is abused, uneducated or goes to bed hungry. It's time to create a world that will not stand for ethnic cleansing, genocide and war. It's time to create a world free of racism, sexism and slavery. It's time to stand up for a world where all peoples can co-exist with mutual respect in a global society where ideas are exchanged freely. It's time for humanity to live up to our potential instead of just praying for it.

It's time for all of us to do whatever we can, whenever we can and wherever we can to make that world a reality. What can you do to help make that world a reality?

The Virtue of Atheists and Non-Believers

I am a person of faith but I have friends who are of many different faiths. I have friends who are Agnostic. I have friends who are non-believers and friends who are atheists. There are many faiths which discourage having friends who are not of the same faith. There are many more faiths which discourage having friendships with atheists. They look at atheists as Godless people. I don't look at atheists that way.

The atheists I know are good people. They love their families. They make sacrifices for their children. They help others. Atheists can test the faith of people of faith. They see people who are good but who do not believe in God and they wonder about why good people will burn in hell for all eternity. These people of faith however, are twisting their religion and giving God base human emotions which are diminishing God.

Non-believers and atheists don't recognize the existence of God. Some are awaiting proof of God's existence because they have not seen any in their lifetime. In truth, evidence of God exists everywhere but your reality is determined by your perception. Two people can see the same thing and see something different based upon their perception.

Let's take, for example, despite the fact that we are a species similar to monkeys and apes, we have built magnificent cities and have invented things like cars, computers and rocket ships. A person of faith look at these things and sees God's hand in them. A non-believer looks at this and sees natural evolution or a series of random events.

A non-believer looks at the horrifying natural and man-made disasters that occur and the disease, poverty and suffering in the world and cites them as proof God does not exist because, if God did exist, how could so many horrible things be allowed to happen? Some of them believe this because, it would be far more horrifying to believe that God does exist but that God is callous and uncaring.

People of faith look at the disasters, disease, poverty and suffering in the world and either see it as punishment, natural occurrences, obstacles or challenges put before us, or as part of God's Mysterious Plan. Others see it as my followers and I do, God's way of sending humanity a message: "Your brothers and sisters are hurting, what are you going to do about it?"

The interesting thing is that People of Faith, Agnostics, Non-Believers and Atheists all choose to help. They all contribute to help the poor, give relief to disaster victims, and cure disease. In so doing, they are acting as Agents of The Lord and replying to God's message "I am helping them".

Those who tell you that non-believers and atheists are going to hell are doing so more out of a need to convert or keep followers to their faith, through fear of eternal damnation then of anything God ever told The Prophets. It has been revealed to me that how you believe in God or whether or not you believe in God makes no difference to God. God is bigger than the human emotion of vengeful pride. Whether or not you believe in God, God believes in you. God is always with you and God communicates with you, through events and through others, whether or not you choose to hear God.

So, rest easy. You don't have to convert to any particular religion because nobody has a monopoly on God. You can believe what you want without fear because God will still love you unconditionally. What culture or family or socio economic status or sexual orientation you were born into are unimportant to God. They are merely what you began with. You have a lifetime to play and learn and grow. The lessons you learn will enrich you, enrich all the lives you touch and enrich God. No matter what your faith, non-belief, or length of your life, we all contribute and in this way, every life has meaning and purpose.

My God

My God doesn't demand people follow orders like robots and doesn't threaten people with eternal damnation to keep them in line because those are egotistical actions and My God isn't egotistical.

My God doesn't punish people for disobeying. My God provides learning opportunities so that they may learn lessons and improve their behavior through a higher understanding instead of out of fear of punishment.

My God doesn't stand silent when people's lives seem to be falling apart, My God communicates with people through The Word, through events and through other people who deliver messages.

My God hasn't given one group of people an exclusive on The Word. My God hasn't reserved an eternal home for the chosen few. My God welcomes everyone who wants to get to know God better.

My God is an equal opportunity lover and loves all living beings equally no matter what form they take. All life is precious to My God and a kindness to any life form is a kindness to God. Taking the life of any life form is taking a part of God that the taker does not have the ability to restore.

My God doesn't judge people by their race, or religion or sexual orientation or economic status because My God knows that these are things all people are born with, a starting point.   My God doesn't look at where you start. My God looks at how you have grown beyond your starting point and what you have learned from the experience we call life.

My God doesn't need pass judgment upon humankind because My God has given a spiritual gene to all people and an objective part of that gene allows all spirits to pass judgment upon themselves.

My God understands that humanity can only understand things when given information they can comprehend. This information is called The Word. My God sends prophets to deliver The Word at times which parallel humanities advancements and ability to understand more. Although God remains the same, The Word is ever changing as new information is added to what humanity knows as humanity has advanced enough to understand it.

My God's will is always done and My God always wins because My God exists in the past, present and future simultaneously. My God is the master of time and can change any outcome, at any time during the past, present or future.

My God has a master plan in which every soul has a role. My God has a mission for each and every person. My God has provided tools for each individual; to find out what their mission is.

My God is your God. My God is the same God you have been praying to no matter what your religion. If you think you know everything about God and you didn't know some or all of these things, do you really know God?

Fulfilling Your Destiny

Every human is born with a destiny. At birth, God whispers the same phrase to every person "The world is a better place because you were born." The phrase is a prophecy. It is a prophecy that proclaims part of your destiny. It is a prophecy you are charged with fulfilling during your lifetime.

Part of your life mission is to find out how your life can fulfill this prophecy.

There are many ways you can fulfill this prophecy. You can fulfill it through a lifetime of service to others. You can fulfill it discovering, creating or inventing something that benefits the world. You can fulfill it by saving the life of another living being.

You can fulfill this part of your destiny through service to others. Many professions, from doctors, to firefighters, to teachers to garbage workers can help fulfill God's prophecy. Most people can understand how doctors, firefighters and teachers are included on the list because doctors and firefighters are perceived as saving lives. Teachers are perceived as saving the future by educating children. Far fewer may understand how a garbage worker can be included on the list. Garbage workers help with diminishing the effects of disease. Many garbage workers become sick from diseases clinging to the refuse of people who are sick. In doing so, they contract an illness that many others might have contracted if the garbage was left out in the open in a public place.

You can fulfill this part of your destiny by discovering, inventing or creating something that benefits humanity. You can discover the cure for a disease. You can invent a machine that helps to clean up the environment. You can create a painting or a sculpture or a poem that uplifts people's spirits or gets them to think about the big questions of life. Any of these types of activities can make the world a better place, one soul at a time.

You can fulfill this part of your destiny by saving the life of another being. Saving the life of a person could enable that person to complete their fulfillment of this part of their destiny. Saving the life of another being, a plant or animal for instance is performing an activity that creates a direct effect for the being you are saving and future generations of that living being's descendants.

Most people are not artists or writers. They cannot create an artistic or literary masterpiece. They are not doctors, or teachers. They live ordinary lives working mundane jobs for less money than they think they are worth. They can save a life, if not the life of a person, then the life of a plant or an animal. They can volunteer to help at a hospital or an orphanage. They can be help a stranger in need, they can join groups like Change Agents for Humanity to get ideas on what they can do.

The question is clear. Will the world be a better place because you were born? The answer may be unclear because in most cases, words alone will not satisfy it. Only your actions will create the answer to the question. What actions are you taking? How is the story of your life answering the question?

Inspiration for All

Selected Inspirational Writings
By The Prophet of Life

A Tribute to Mothers

When so many fathers are not around

The head of the family is the mother

No Matter what language you speak

Mother Is spelled LOVE

Where would you be without your mother?

You would not be here.

In many cultures mothers are seen as the child bearers

But in reality they are the Life Givers

Because they not only bear children but nurture and raise them as well

And for many, a mother's love is the only human love that is unconditional

And the only love from another human being that has endured throughout their lives

Even those who don't know who their father is know who their mother is

So if your mother is alive

Hug her

If she is far away, call her

You know she would always do the same for you

If she has passed on

Remember her

Say a prayer for her

She may not have been perfect

But she always did the best she could

I will close with lyrics about mothers

From a song I wrote Called "Hope Is The Answer"

Woman is a mother

She's got a lot of mouths to feed

Feels like a martyr

Frustration is what she bleeds

So many disappointments

Yet her faith it keeps her strong

Kids need someone to look up to

In times of desperation

Fatherhood

Every, June 21st it's Father's Day in America. Having spent time in America, I will take this day to write about fatherhood. My father left my mother after their divorce. My sister and I spent many years growing up in foster homes. I had no real father figure to look up to. I gravitated towards men who had qualities I admired so I could observe them and learn what manhood was about. A neighbor taught me how to tie a tie. A teacher taught me the importance of written expression. A boss taught me the importance of courtesy and developing a work ethic. All of these temporary surrogate fathers made an impact on me.

Then one day, I realized that there had always been one father figure present in my life all along. God. I know now that God is neither male nor female but when I was young, I needed a father figure, so for these purposes, God was a male. I thought about the kindness God bestows upon all beings. I worked on developing my innate kindness. I thought about how God works to right wrongs and I endeavored to use my writing ability as a tool to help right the wrongs in this world. I thought about how God loves all living beings and developed a sense of love for all things, people, animals, plants and even bugs.

I have known many men in my life. Some have abandoned their children. Others are excellent fathers. I try and influence those who have abandoned their children into get back into their children's lives in any way they are able. I frequently praise the fathers who are excellent fathers. I really admire them. I applaud them. While they believe that they are doing a wonderful thing for their family, they are also doing a wonderful thing for humanity. Through parenting, they are shaping the future of humanity by developing great people who will contribute to humanity. Above all, they are doing God's work.

Fathers are special people. Any man can be a sperm donor. It takes a great man to take the time, effort and devotion to be a father. To all the great fathers out there you are appreciated. Enjoy your day.

The Best Gift To Give a Child.

What is the best gift to give a child?
It's not something you have to spend a lot of money on.
It is something you will have to spend time on.
The best gift to give a child is the gift of high positive self-esteem.
Girls with high positive self-esteem are less likely to sleep around and become pregnant in their teen years.
Boys who have high positive self-esteem are less likely to become victims of bullying.
Kids who have high positive self-esteem are less likely to succumb to peer pressure become drug addicted or gang members
And are more likely to believe in themselves and not afraid to think out of the box or act independently.
All of these things are benchmarks of success in school, in work and in life.
Positive High Self-esteem can be built by:
Praising the good things your child does.

Encouraging your child to try new things.
Supporting the things you child wants to try and to do.
Showing your child unconditional love no matter what they have done.
So save your money.
Take the time
Make the effort.
Give your child positive high self-esteem.

Muscle Man

A husband and wife had been married for many years. The husband had long since passed his prime and rarely exercised. He still liked to think of himself as a handsome, well-built man. One day, his wife touched his belly, which had expanded several inches over the years, and said "Flabby".

The man took this statement to heart and resolved to do some-thing about it. He detested exercise. The next time he saw her hand move towards him he tensed his muscles. She didn't say he was flabby. Over time, the man developed the habit of tensing up whenever his wife's hand moved towards his body.

One day the wife decided to test her husband. She moved her hand towards his shoulder, he tensed up. It was rock hard. She moved her hand towards his arm. He tensed up there too, she giggled. She moved her hand to the small of his back, he tensed up there too. She giggled again. Her hand gently roamed toward the back of his thigh. He tensed up there too. She laughed.

Then, with a twinkle in his eye, he said "How do you like your muscle man?"

"I wish the man I was feeling was the man I was married to." She replied with a smirk.

Give Love

Give the gift that keeps on giving
Give love

Give birth to a feeling that will keep on giving
Give love

Give the kind of gift
That money can't buy

The only one that guaranteed
To satisfy

Give love
This time, give love

You don't have to fight through traffic
Or wait in long lines

To give the gift that will be cherished
For a whole life time

Give love

Give the gift that's right for every occasion
That's a beautiful expression

Of your own creation

Give love
This time give love

If you care enough to give the very best
There's no reason to settle for less

Give love

A Smart Spouse

Bryan and Annie had been married about four years. Bryan was fifteen years older than 27 year old Annie. Annie and Bryan had a big dog. Annie had the habit of allowing the dog to climb up on her lap, touch his nose to hers and give her a big lick on her face. Bryan never really minded it. It was just one of those peculiar things a spouse does that the other spouse put up with and learns to ignore.

Annie's mother was visiting for a week. She worked very hard making a turkey dinner. The three of them sat down at the table and began eating. Suddenly, their dog Sparky put his front paws on Annie's lap and hoisted himself up. She turned her face towards him and he touched his nose to hers. Then he give her face a great big lick. The dog lowered himself down and laid down besides Annie.

Annie's mother was horrified by what she had just witnessed.

"What a pig!" she yelled. "What a pig you are Annie!"

Then she looked at Bryan. "What do you think boychic? Which of them is a pig, your dog or my daughter?"

Bryan thought for a moment before he responded.

"If you're asking me which one is a pig, my wife or my dog, the pig is always my dog." He said.

Annie chuckled with glee. "What a wonderful husband I have!"

Annie's mother quipped "But Annie is intelligent she has a brain and should know better. The dog is just a dumb dog?"

"Because tonight, when I go to sleep," Bryan replied, "I want to sleep in my bed with my beautiful, loving wife instead of in the doghouse with Sparky."

One Small Candle

VERSE 1

She lived in the middle of the city
But felt like she was living in hell
She wondered how she ended up here
And felt dread as the night fell
She felt so isolated
And scarred by broken dreams
She fell asleep serenaded by
Gunshots, moans and screams
They lit one small candle
And put it next to her window
To fight against the darkness
And let the world know
That one small candle
One soul to stand for right
One small candle
To keep away the night

As she struggled every day
To walk towards her goals while surrounded by
Those who lost their way
She was assaulted by temptations
Hammered by neglect

But kept on walking anyway
One step following the next
She lit one small candle

This went on for years
And things got better over time
She struggled every day
And lit a candle every night
One night before turning in
She looked out and to her surprise
Saw 10,000 other candles
Drowning the darkness with their light

They lit one small candle
And put it next to her window
To fight against the darkness
And let the world know
That one small candle
One soul to stand for right
One small candle
To keep away the night

"Many Hands Make Light Work."

Joe was a farmer. He had a wife and two children. He had a 400 acre farm. Joe had many duties to fulfill on his farm. He had to tend to his corn crop, He had to tend to his herd of 10 cows and four horses. He had to feed his 30 chickens and 8 pigs. Joe's day began at 5:00 a.m. and often didn't end until 6:00 p.m.

Even though Joe had a lot of work to do on his farm, he never hesitated to help a neighbor in need. When the Johnson family needed some feed for their chickens to tide them over one winter, Joe gave them some of his feed. When the Perez family's grazing land burned down he let them graze their three cows with his 10. When the Umboogoo family's eldest son broke his leg on their farm, Joe helped set it and drove him to the nearest doctor in Factoryville 75 miles away.

One day, a tornado hit the area where Joe and his family lived. It churned and turned and whirled in a very scary way. It tore up various sections of land in the farms all around Joe's Family Farm. The tornado destroyed Joe's barn. The next morning, Joe cut down some trees and began sawing planks to rebuild his barn. He estimated it would take him a month to cut the word and build his barn. With winter due to begin in a week, that was bad news for Joe.

Two days passed, Joe's neighbors found out about Joe's barn. They knew he wouldn't be able to build it in time for winter. All of the family farmers that lived near Joe thought about the nice things Joe had done for them. On the morning of the third day, 60 people showed up to help Joe rebuild his barn. Within two days a brand new barn stood where the old one had lay in ruins a few days before. If Joe had to build that barn by himself it would have been impossible for him to finish it on time. With the help of many of his friends, the barn was finished on time. This chapter in Joe's life taught him the meaning of the maxim "Many hands make light work."

Nelson Mandela How One Life Can Change The World

Although he was not from America, Nelson Mandela grew up in a segregated society where racists ran the government. His remarkable story serves as an inspiration to those struggling with racism today.

Nelson Mandela was born to the Thembu Royal Family of the Xhosa tribe in South Africa in 1918. He studied law at a university. When he was an adult he moved to Johannesburg and ran head on into apartheid South Africa's version of institutional racism). Although Black people were in the majority in South Africa, they couldn't vote, had to live in segregated areas and their movements and speech were restricted.

Mandela joined the African National Congress (ANC) and anti-apartheid organization. In 1948 The Afrikaner Nationalist Party took over South Africa and moved to strengthen apartheid. Over the next 14 years, Mandela rose in prominence and became a leader in the ANC. In 1962 he was put on trial for conspiracy to overthrow the Government of South Africa and was sentenced to life in prison.

He spent most of the next 27 years at a prison on Robben Island off the coast of South Africa. An international effort lobbied for Mandela's release from prison. He was released n in 1990. Mandela became President of the ANC and over the next four years, he negotiated with South African President F.W. De Klerk to abolish apartheid and hold South Africa's first multi-racial elections. In 1993 he won the Nobel peace Prize and in 1994 he was elected President of South Africa. During his term in office he found a way to create a bridge between the races and made South Africa a prosperous nation of true equality. He led by example and illustrated how one life can change the world.

When Mandela was imprisoned the end of apartheid seemed an insurmountable goal. Yet he envisioned it. He was deprived of his liberty by a government that imprisoned him for much of his life yet he forgave his jailers and overcame their prison. He chipped away at the rock hard resolve of apartheid until it crumbled beneath the weight of his righteousness. Once in power, he didn't take vengeance but built bridges and with wisdom and courage, made South Africa the model for other nations and became an inspiration for all of humanity.

Teenage Mysteries of Life Solved.

You know how your parents are always telling you not to do things, but they never tell you why? They tell you things like work hard, get good grades, respect others, be careful of the company you keep and stay away from drugs and alcohol. All your mysteries are about to be solved. This article is going to tell you why.

Parents tell you to work hard and get good grades because, for most societies across the globe, school is the path to upward mobility. Even the poorest of people from the poorest of families can move upward economically, socially and intellectually by getting a good education. Going to a good school can help you develop into a more disciplined, well versed, well rounded person. Going to the right school could get you powerful connections that will help you advance in the future. People without money or connections can get into the right school but only through excellent grades. Graduating will be the key to a good job. A good job is the key to economic advancement.

Parents tell you to respect others. They tell you this because people who don't respect others don't get respect themselves. If you get a job and don't show your colleagues and customers respect you won't have a job for long. Gangsters and criminals don't get respect. They think they do but what they actually get is fake respect to their faces while people are laughing at them behind their back. This is because they have no job and no future. They don't respect anyone. They give intimidation through fear and have to carry a weapon to get the fear. That's pretty sad.

Parents tell you to be careful of the company you keep. This is because you are judged by the company you keep. If you hang around with the brainiacs, people think you are one of them. People will think you are smart. If you hang around people who curse a lot, you will end up cussing a lot. If you hang around thugs, people think you are a thug or a wanna be thug. When thugs are attacked by rivals guess who else suffers the consequences? You do. While the thugs have other thugs for backup, you've got nobody. If thugs commit crimes, and you hang with them you automatically become a suspect. Suspects can sometimes be arrested ad even charged with a crime. Even if you aren't convicted, you may still get a reputation. One that may follow you into your adult life.

Parents tell you to stay away from drugs and alcohol. This is because drugs and alcohol are addictive. They can become the focus of your life while everything else, including more important things fall by the wayside. It's difficult to concentrate in school when you are high. If you can't concentrate, you can't pass classes. If you can't pass classes, you can't graduate. If you don't graduate, you can't get a decent job. Before you know it, you will be in the workforce. If you are high all the time you won't be able to keep a job. If you already have a reputation and even a nick name that indicates you are a druggie, it's likely that it will follow you into the world of work. Who is going to hire a drug addict?

There are reasons that your parents tell you these things. They may not tell you. Perhaps they don't know how to tell you. The reasons may not be clear to them but the reasons are clear and they make logical sense. They are all based on caring. Your parents care about your future. They only want the best for you. They have lived longer than you and have more experiences with life than you do. They have learned from their own mistakes or from the mistakes of their friends. They may see you making some of the same mistakes and they are trying to save you the aggravation of suffering the consequences of those mistakes.

Hope Is The Answer

VERSE 1

Man is an employee
Working and sweating every single day
Doesn't have much money
Still he's got bills to pay
He questions the master
And has a long wait for his reply
Just when He's going to give up
Comes the revelation
That hope is the answer
When all else fades away

VERSE 2

Woman is a mother
She's got a lot of mouths to feed
Feels like a martyr
Frustration is what she bleeds
So many disappointments
Yet her faith it keeps her strong
Kids need someone to look up to
In times of desperation
Hope is the answer

VERSE 3

So much suffering and heartache
Bourne upon this worldly plain
So many caught up in it
That can't see beyond their pain
Cries the Wisdom of the ages
All wounds are healed in time
Like a beacon to the future
Shines the inspiration
That Hope is the answer

The True Meaning of Failure

"Success often arrives on the coattails of failure."

Have you ever failed at anything? Of course you have. If you are like most people, failure is a common occurrence. Not because everybody completely sucks but because failure is a part of the learning process. If you are like me, you probably fail at most new things you try. If you keep on trying however, you get better.

Do you know how to walk? Can you talk? These are things you learned as a baby. When you were a baby, you took your first few steps and fell and fell again but you kept on trying. You were likely curious about this new mode of transportation your mommy and daddy were using.

What would have happened if you gave up on walking? Can you imagine what your life would be like if you had to crawl everywhere? You didn't give up. You kept on trying and learning from your mistakes and making correction and now, you are walking like a champ!

There can be no success without failure. Success is often a matter of trial and error. What scientists call error, the rest of us call failure. Failure is an opportunity to learn. You learn what doesn't work. You can either believe that the whole thing doesn't work, you can't do it and likely never will and give up or you can try another way.

Failure can be the key that unlocks the door to success. Besides learning what doesn't work, failure can teach you what went wrong and why it went wrong. If you analyze a failure and trace all of the steps you took leading up to it, you can see just where you went wrong and once you knowing where you went wrong often leads to knowing how and why you went wrong. Knowing where, how and why you went wrong can give you information that allows you to make corrections, corrections that will lead to adjustments that in time will lead to success. The information yielded from failure can be the keys that unlock the door to success.

A Matter of Perspective

Three old men were sitting on a bus bench. To pass the time they had a conversation comparing how hard their childhoods were. While the first two old men were talking, the third just sat listening.

The first old man said "When I a kid, I had to walk three miles to school every morning."

The second old man said "I had to walk four miles."

The first old man said "There were no traffic signals, I risked my life crossing the street."

The second old man said: "You had streets? I had dirt roads. I risked my life with every step I took because a car could run me over at any time."

The first old man, who was by now upset said: "I had to walk in sub-zero, freezing temperatures!"

The second old man said "I did too and our weather was so cold, my jacket froze!"

The first old man, figuring out how the second old man bested him, chimed in: "You had Jackets!"

The second old man replied: "Yes we had jackets but we were so poor my jacket was made out of paper bags."

The first old man, in an obviously lame attempt to best the second one, shouted: "Yeah? Well, when I was a kid I walked to school in temperatures so cold my shoes froze!"

To which the second old man replied: "You had shoes?"

The Third old man, who had been sitting quietly during the entire conversation suddenly spoke; "You had feet?"

Then he opened his jacket and revealed two legs cut off at the knee caps.

Sometimes we look at life from the perspectives of our own problems and in so doing, ignore how fortunate we really are.

Inspiratio nal Quotes

"Imagination is the jet fuel that uplifts humanity."
"Those who have done the impossible often didn't know it was impossible when they did it."
The Prophet of Life Memorial Tribute to Steve Jobs, You Tube Video

Everybody makes a difference.

When your world is collapsing all around you, it is time to reinvent yourself.

"Leadership is a collaborative endeavor."
"Of all the souls who have ever lived, you have been chosen to live in these times." 2012 New Years Message you tube video
"When your life is a constant series of miracles, every moment becomes your greatest moment, until the next one happens."

"The world is changed by simple ideas put into practice." The Prophet of Life
from: Revelations of 2012, The Path of Possibilities
ISBN # 978-1-93646200-1
"A new day is dawning there is a revolution in the psyche of humanity." The Prophet of Life
from: Revelations of 2012, The Path of Possibilities
ISBN # 978-1-93646200-1

"Persistence can melt away resistance."

"Incremental planning and sustained execution can make the insurmountable possible."

"Courage is the ability to act in spite of fear."
"Failure is not truly failure unless you fail to learn from it."

"Work can turn dreams into reality."
"Planning can make dreams into reality."
"Having a goal can make dreams into reality."
"Incremental planning and sustained execution can make the insurmountable possible."
The balance of mind, body and spirit is the key to preventing and curing disease.

We can work together as one race, the human race to heal the planet, heal the food chain and heal ourselves in the process. The time for selfish thinking is over. The time for thinking globally and acting locally is in the middle of its tenure. The time for thinking and acting cooperatively is about to dawn.

The solution to our problems does not lie in the knowledge and resources of any one culture or nation but in the knowledge and resources of all of them, both ancient and modern. We have the power to determine our future. Our actions today will determine our benefits or consequences tomorrow. Be it feast or famine, the future shall be a heaven or hell of our own making.

"Even the poorest among us deserve the dignity of equality." The Prophet of Life

From Inspirational Quotes by The prophet of Life
You Tube video

Miracles are vision that supersedes reality.

Miracles happen when vision supersedes reality.
Positive motivation is the life force of an
enlightened generation

The attitude of "Yes I Can" works best when
you've got a plan.

Every life is precious. Every life is important.
Every life has a purpose.

"No Matter what language you speak, Mother Is
spelled LOVE
Where would you be without your mother? You
would not be here."

From the book "True Stories of Inspiration and
General Interest" by The Prophet of Life

Quotes about God

By The Prophet of Life

His quotes have been used by institutions of higher learning, Institutions of medicine, The Occupy Movement, Charities, Businesses and common people around the globe. Although he has a birth name, to many across the globe he is known as The Prophet of Life. Now Love Force International brings you a series of books on his quotes by subject.

Preface
I've always liked quotes. Quotes are like little gems of language that say a lot with just a few words. Sometimes they are humorous, other times they are profound. Good quotes can open up worlds of thought and contemplation. They can explain things that one might have previously not been able to comprehend. I particularly like one line quotes that summarize a mood, theme or a concept. I have also written The Best Spiritual Quotes and The Best Quotes on Gen Topics.

This book is filled with quotes I have developed over the past 20 years. My production of quotes really skyrocketed after I began blogging (after 2006), because my writing production increased. As a part of blogging, I have read and commented on other people's blogs. On a website dedicated to my writings: www.prophetoflife.com, a You Tube site: https://www.youtube.com/user/thetrueprophetofli fe   and my blog: https://edgeucationnewmedia.wordpress.com/cate gory/insight-a-blog-by-the-prophet-of-life, I have had dialogue with others who have either read, or viewed my writings. All of these things have not only stimulated my writing production, they have created quotes.

Many of the quotes in this book are from blogs, stories and other things I have written. Others are stand-alone quotes which I developed to capture a particular sentiment. I have included quotes on popular topics such as God, Faith, Life, Love and Spirituality among others. It is my hope that my quotes will open my readers to worlds of thought and inspire and help them understand things at a deeper level. Purchasing this book gives you a limited license to use any of the quotes in this book for personal use on a non-commercial basis as long as you attribute whatever you use to The Prophet of Life. Use outside of this limited license may be considered copyright infringement and could be punishable to a fine of up to $500.00 per item the copyrighted material appears on and / or in. Uses under this license include such things as using a quote to close an email, on a letter, in a report, or on your website. The proper way to use it is as follows:

"Since everyone is worthy of God's love, no one is worthless." ---The Prophet of Life

"People often wonder why God allows hunger, poverty and war in our world. Perhaps God wonders why we allow it."

"For The Lord so loved all of life, that all of life was imbued with a piece of The Lord."

"Humanity trying to comprehend the nature of God is like an ant trying to comprehend a forest the size of North America."

"The reason humankind has trouble comprehending God is due to the fact that there is a difference between human time and God time. Most humans exist in the present. God exists in the past, present and future simultaneously."

"People rarely see the effects they have on the people whose lives they touch but The Lord does."

"What is God? God is beyond human kind's ability to define God. The real question is: What is God to you?"

"There are many ways to define God. Some definitions are collective and others are individual."

"To save a life, any life, be it animal, vegetable or human is an act on behalf of The Lord."

"All life is precious and every life has a purpose unto God."

"Rejoice Humanity, for a new day has dawned and the hour of your liberation is upon you. The truth that shall set you free is inscribed into your spiritual DNA. The Lord is, has and always will be with you. Every living being has something to contribute. Every living being plays an important role in the final history. Every soul is important and every soul makes a difference. The time to fear God is over. The time to understand God has begun. This is not the beginning of the end but it is the end of the beginning." The Prophet of Life from Revelations of 2012, The Path of Possibilities, ISBN# 978-1-93646200-1

"A good many humans, judge others not based on God's Law but based on the perception of God's Laws that we have been raised to believe or through study or experience have come to believe."

"The more you come to know The Lord you find out just how unqualified you are to pass judgment on anyone."

"God is a Master Teacher and everyone and everything put in your life is put there to teach a lesson in the spiritual school we call life."

"Everything is part of God's plan. Even the people and things they do that seem to go against God."

"Since God is a universal God, and since there are living beings on many other planets, the souls of all of these beings populate heaven as well as those from our planet. These souls and the beings they are incarnated as also enjoy the blessings of The Lord's Love and Grace. Everything that has been revealed in this book of Revelations holds true for our planet but because God is a Lord of all that is and ever was, all that exists, has existed and will exist, most things within this book are true for other planets and populations as well."

"God's Word, The Word is not ever changing. The ability of humankind to comprehend it accurately comes in increments over generations and decades and centuries and millennia."

"Some people wonder why God abandoned them or their loved ones in their time of need. Some people lose their faith as a result of things that they perceive God allowed to happen to them. That is just their perception. In truth, God never abandons anyone."

"God is a part of all of us and we are all a part of God."

"The Lord is not ever changing, humanity's ability to understand that which is The Lord evolves in increments over long periods of time." From **The Tenants of Revelations of 2012**

"It is true, the spirit of God does permeate all we do including the lessons we are taught by the difficulties we encounter in our lives."

"Since all of life is endowed with a part of The Lord to take a life is to take part of The Lord. To save a life is to save a part of The Lord."

"The reason humankind has trouble comprehending God is due to the fact that there is a difference between human time and God time. Most humans exist in the present. God exists in the past, present and future simultaneously. Think of it as a three level chess set. Humanity plays on one level and only one level. God plays on all three levels simultaneously. The ramifications for humanity in regards to our knowledge and experience base are profound. They are as profound as our relative limitations."

"The Lord talks to everyone but most people do not know how to listen."

"Your belief in God is not a prerequisite for God believing in you."

"God is not a religion. Religion is humanity trying to understand God."

"As each soul brings what it has learned from its life experience, that which is God is enriched but the soul that comes to God is not the soul you have lived with, it is the soul you were born with, enriched by your life experience but not tainted by it. God does not evolve, neither does the soul you were born with as they are a constant and evolved far beyond human beings."

"For God so loves all of life that all of life is endowed with a part of The Lord in their spiritual DNA." The Prophet of Life from Revelations of 2012, The Path of Possibilities, ISBN# 978-1-93646200-1

"How often is it that modern "Revelations are similar or rehashed ancient truths? Very often. This is because The Lord is revealed to humanity in increments over long periods of time. That is also why the world's five great faiths have so many similar messages because The Lord keeps repeating the same messages in different ways. Once humanity realizes this, there will be less need for those of different faiths to dehumanize one another, learn to respect those who believe differently and work together to make an authentic positive change in the world possible."

The Lord doesn't make mistakes.
The mistake is in the perception
which is often based on limited
information. from the Kindle book: Finding God
in A Chaotic World, ISBN# 978-1-936462-01-8

"God's love is beyond all of
the horrible, cruel things
done by humanity."

"Most humans exist in the present. God exists in the past, present and future simultaneously. Think of it as a three level chess set. Humanity plays on one level and only one level. God plays on all three levels simultaneously. The ramifications for humanity in regards to our knowledge and experience base are profound. They are as profound as our relative limitations. Humankind trying to comprehend God is like an ant trying to comprehend a forest the size of North America."

"Everyone and everything serves God's purpose. Even those who act badly serve as bad examples. In this way, everyone plays a part in the lives of everyone they touch."

"Since everyone is worthy of God's love, No one is worthless."

From the You Tube Video Inspirational Quotes by The Prophet of Life

"It is only God that exists in the past, present and future simultaneously. We have only the present."

"Most humans exist in the present. God exists in the past, present and future simultaneously. Think of it as a three level chess set. Humanity plays on one level and only one level. God plays on all three levels simultaneously. The ramifications for humanity in regards to our knowledge and experience base are profound. They are as profound as our relative limitations. Humankind trying to comprehend God is like an ant trying to comprehend a forest the size of North America."

"God is justice, God is compassion. God is beyond all things that you can imagine. God is love." From the song God Is Love by The Prophet of Life

"The Path of our life experience continues beyond death and all that is gained through life experience is returned to The Lord."

"My God doesn't punish people for disobeying. My God provides learning opportunities so that they may learn lessons and improve their behavior through a higher understanding instead of out of fear of punishment." From the Kindle Book: Finding God in A Chaotic World

"God is a universal God. Living Beings on all planets and in all galaxies know of God."

"The ultimate cosmic joke is that there is no one right way. The Lord is so incomprehensible that knowledge of The Lord can be revealed over long periods of time. That is why The Lord sends Prophets with long stretches of time in between them instead of all at once, because The Lord only reveals something to us when we have advanced enough to begin to comprehend it. That is just this planet. Multiply that by the thousands of planets in the universe where life exists and you begin to see the compounded irony of the one true way mentality. I have found that often, when a religion says that their way is the only way, it is more a reflection of a fear of losing followers or a desire to remain relevant than something that actually comes from The Lord.

"God exists where life is present."

"You don't have to be religious to find God because religion is not God, it is man's interpretation of God. In reality God communicates with everyone including you, it is just that many people either aren't aware of this or don't know "how" God communicates with them so they don't think it is God that is communicating. Many people join a religion because they need the structure or because they want to be "saved" and many religions tell you they have an exclusive path to God. This is not true. Religions usually are founded based on the teachings of a particular prophet. God reveals that which is God to humanity in increments over long periods of time that correspond with humanities development. Humanity gets what it needs and we learn a little more each time. So go ahead and join your church but remember the church is not God. If you want to find God search within yourself and look at your life and figure out when God has been communicating with you and what those messages were."

"God exists in the past, present and future simultaneously. The opposition only exists in the present."

"When I helplessly witnessed the disintegration of my parent's marriage and was placed in the homes of strangers who repeatedly abused me, I learned lessons and developed compassion for those who suffered similarly. When I became a responsible adult, I helped them and served as an example that it was possible to come out of that hell and still lead a normal life. God was there." From the Kindle book: What Faith Has Taught Me

"God's love is beyond all of the horrible, cruel things done by humanity."

"My God doesn't stand silent when people's lives seem to be falling apart, My God communicates with people through The Word, through events and through other people who deliver messages."

"In the entirety of the history of humanity God has created only one you. You are unique and you have a special purpose. Remember that when you feel depressed or worthless.

"Every human is born with a destiny. At birth, God whispers the same phrase to every person "The world is a better place because you were born." The phrase is a prophecy. It is a prophecy that proclaims part of your destiny. It is a prophecy you are charged with fulfilling during your lifetime." From the Kindle book What Faith Has Taught Me

"Those who perform an act of kindness have the power to bestow the blessings of The Lord. The blessing is bestowed upon both the giver and the receiver."

"Since the dawn of time wars have been fought in the name of God. In reality, they weren't fought for God at all. They were fought to defend or expand somebody's version God."

"It is true, the spirit of God does permeate all we do including the lessons we are taught by the difficulties we encounter in our lives."

The Lord doesn't make mistakes. The mistake is in the perception which is often based on limited information. from the Kindle book: Finding God in A Chaotic World, ISBN# 978-1-936462-01-8

Author Biography
The Prophet of Life

I am a journalist, author and songwriter. I write the Faith and Spiritual books as well as topical, thematic literature books for Love Force International Publishing.

I have had very broad and varied life experiences and those experiences enrich my writing. I write on Spiritual topics as well as topics of global importance. I write non-fiction that tells it like it is but that is solution oriented as opposed to just complaining about things. I have books on topics such as Crime and Punishment, Racism, and Faith.

I like writing things from unique perspectives. I like to challenge my reader's perceptions and allow them to come away with new insights. If a lesson can be woven into the fabric of the written word, so much the better but the lesson is often subtle.

I try and see things the way they are and the way that they can be. This allows me to see the possibilities within various situations both in my life and in the things I write. As a result, I can often add twists and turns readers will not likely see coming in fiction I write. I can often communicate things from unique and different perspectives and see solutions to problems and issues that I communicate about in my nonfiction.

I am not afraid to take risks both in my life and in

my writing. I have tackled controversial issues in both. My nonfiction Word Press blog, Insight, a blog by The Prophet of Life, is full of examples. I have an offbeat sense of humor and have written humorous things as well as serious. I started a You Tube Channel and now have over 100 videos that have words and music but no pictures. Despite the fact that there are no pictures over 150,000 people from 210 different nations have viewed the videos on my You Tube channel.

I enjoy hearing from my readers. I enjoy writing. I hope you will find my books interesting and entertaining.

Kindle Books by The Prophet of Life Include: (Followed by SP = Spanish Version available, followed by ppr = Available on paperback only)
The Prophet of Life Reader, Volume 1 SP
The Prophet of Life Reader Volume 2 SP
Black in America
Controversy SP
Every Lyric Tells A Story SP
Finding God in A Chaotic World SP
Finding God Without Religion, An agnostic path to God SP
Inspiration for All 1 Inspiration for your spirit SP
Inspiration for All 2 Inspiration for your mind SP
Life Success Kit SP
Reflections in The Mirror of Life

Romance Lives!
The Best Quotes about God SP
The Best Spiritual Quotes   SP
The Best Quotes About Topics of General Interest SP
The Faith Trilogy ppr   SP
The Agnostic Faith Trilogy ppr SP
True Stories   SP
True Stories of Crime and Punishment SP
True Stories of Inspiration and General Interest SP
What Faith Has Taught Me SP

Kindle Books by Loveforce International Publishing

Whether you are interested in true stories, fiction, humor, action, adventure, spiritual insights, quotes, poetry, self-help or children's books, Loveforce International Publishing has got you covered. **Our 99 cent commitment,** our commitment to a 99 cent (U.S.) price for all our kindle e book titles keep our books affordable. Since our books sell for the local equivalent of 99 cents (U.S.) in other global markets, people around the globe can afford them. Our books do sell all over the world. Our 99 cent commitment means there has never been a better time to stock up on books published by Love Force International! At a time when many paperbacks sell for $13.95-$17.95, our paperbacks sell for between $6.50-$7.50 (U.S.). This too is a bargain for our readers.

Many of the books listed here include their Amazon Kindle ASIN code. Typing an ASIN code into any Amazon search bar should bring that title up. If you are looking for titles published by Loveforce International Publishing you can simply type Loveforce International Publishing Company into any amazon search bar anywhere in the world and many of our books will come up. For books in Spanish type Loveforce Libros en Espanol into any Amazon search bar anywhere in the world.

Many of our books have Spanish Language versions. We didn't just slap the text onto Google Translate and pray. We worked with a professional Spanish translator born and raised in a Spanish speaking nation. We made our authors available to that person to clarify idioms and other translation glitches so that our Spanish versions are not only close to the original in meaning but they also fit within the culture(s) of Spanish Speaking nations.

We have some promotional videos for our books on Amazon Kindle. You can find many others on our You Tube channel The Loveforce International Publishing channel. Just type Loveforce International Publishing into your You Tube search bar anywhere in the world and the channel will come up along with many of our videos. Our logo is a photo of the sun coming out through a cloud over a mountain top. We have a Spanish Language You Tube Channel as well. Type Loveforce International Publishing en Espanol and you will see some of our Spanish language videos from our Loveforce enEspanol channel come up with the ones in English.

NOTE: Books with ASINs are available now the others will be available soon. All Titles are printed in English. Books with an **SP** after the title also have a version translated into Spanish. A List of Paperbacks will be below, Reader Series books with a paperback version will have **Ppr** on the same line as the title.

The Reader Series is a series of readers that are a sampling of writings by one or more authors.

The Prophet of Life Reader (7 Book Sampler) Volumes 1 & 2
What do essays, articles, stories, poetry and quotes have in common? They are all in this sampling of stories, poems and other writings from 7 of The Prophet of Life's writings found in these Kindle books.
Author: The Prophet of Life   **ISBN: 978-1-936462-07-0**
ASIN: B015D716C0 (Vol 1)   ASIN: B06XBSWKX8 (Vol 2)

The Mark Wilkins Reader 7 Book Sampler! Volumes 1 & 2
One story from seven books by Mark Wilkins. Whether its smart spouses, inquisitive fools, teachers, gangsters or ghosts these books give you a good sampling of stories by the man known throughout the world as A Storyteller. Within its pages you will find horror, humor and pathos.
 Author: Mark Wilkins   **ISBN: 978-1-936462-38-4**
ASIN: B01MU0Z51H Volume 1

The Love Force International Reader 7 Book Sampler! 4 Books in This Series

Whether you want fiction, humor, children's stories, poetry or quotes these books have got all of those and more! A sampling of 7 different books by three authors offered in Kindle books published by Love Force International.
Edited by Evan Lovefire   Vol 1 **ASIN:** B06XBHD9RX
Vol 2 **ASIN:** B06XBMGLNK
Vol 3 ASIN: B07DCGTLKF   Vol 4
ASIN: B07DP51BWG

The Love Force International Sampler, Spanish Books Edition SP Volumes 1 & 2
These books contain a sampling of 7 different books by three authors translated into Spanish. The books translated include What Faith has Taught me, Controversy, True Stories of Inspiration & General interest and Quotes about God by The Prophet of Life, Stories of The Supernatural, Slices of Life How to Become The Person You've Always Wanted by Mark Wilkins and Classic Children's Stories You've Likely Never Heard, and my first & second books of stupid little fables by Dr. Goose.
Edited by C. Gomez Vol 1 **ASIN:** B06XB3RJ2K Vol 2
ASIN:: B07F2PLVHF

The True Stories Series is a series of books which include true stories.

True Stories!   SP
A riveting collection of true stories. Whether you want to know about the toddler taken by a gator at a Disney Resort, an 18 year old who doesn't exist, which popular restaurant chain has a corporate mentality of public humiliation for its employees or an alarming new trend that could affect your household this book has got it all and they are all absolutely true!
Author: The Prophet of Life   **ISBN: 978-1-936462-16-2**
ASIN: B06XVSZSZ9

True Stories: Inspiration and General Interest
SP
What do cell phone addicts, George Orwell, birds, Paul McCartney, The Nobel Prize, Black Friday, Led Zeppelin, garbage, a pep talk, tipping, Steve Jobs, Shakespeare, inspirational thoughts and your mother have in common? They are in true stories in this book. True Stories of Inspiration & General Interest brings together stories and poems about celebrities, trends and everyday people. Sometimes surprising, always interesting, it will entertain you and give you something to think about at the same time.
Author: The Prophet of Life   **ISBN: 978-1-936462-15-5**
ASIN: B00TXWVNUC   ASIN: B01BBCKFZU
(Spanish Edition)

Controversy

Ppr SP

What do Caitlyn Jenner, Donald Trump, a cure for AIDS, Chinese hackers, Adolf Hitler and Global Warming have in common? They are all at the heart of a controversy and there are stories about them in this unique book that turns tabloid headlines inside out. **Author:** The Prophet of Life **ISBN: 978-1-936462-19-3** ASIN: B016MWU8NS **ASIN: B01CRF3098 (Spanish Edition)**

True Stories of Crime and Punishment

SP

This book of serious crime stories is ripped from headlines all over the globe. From the family that vanished, to the 11 year old girl killed in a fight over a boy, to the prisoner who hasn't eaten in 14 years, to the severed human head found near the famous Hollywood sign these stories ripped will astound you and give you pause to think.
Author: The Prophet of Life **ISBN: 978-1-936462-17-9 ASIN: B01406YZBE ASIN: B01N10ND7S (Spanish Edition)**

Strange but True!

A collection of facts and stories about people, places and things that are strange and seem like fiction but are absolutely true!

Author: Mark Wilkins **ASIN:**

The A Storyteller Series is a unique book series. Instead of concentrating on a particular character or genre, the series consists of collections of short stories by Author Mark Wilkins, Also Known As A Storyteller.

The Slice of Life Series are books with humorous stories.

Slices of Life Volume 1
                   SP
is a collection of humorous short stories about life. Most of them deal with marriage and family members. From smart spouses to intelligent little children to guys trying to impress their friends and in-laws trying to master technology each story is like a little slice of life but together, they make up an irresistible pie. Sit back, grab a cup of coffee and enjoy some slices of lie because, before you know it, you will have finished the whole thing.
Author: Mark Wilkins **ISBN: 978-1-936462-11-7 ASIN: B014ZF5VY0   ASIN: B01BBBZUL0 (Spanish Edition)**

Slices of Life Volume 2
                   SP
This sequel to Slices of Life has more humorous stories about the rich, the poor and the middle class. It even has a story about one of their pets. Ignorance is the main theme of this book, ignorance that has consequences that are sometimes touching but always humorous. So brew so coffee or tea, sit down and relax and enjoy another satisfying batch of more slice of life because, before you know it, you will have devoured the whole thing.

Author: Mark Wilkins **ISBN:** 978-1-936462-12-4 **ASIN:** B01M2B3YZ1 **ASIN:** B06XKP5C66 (Spanish Edition)

The Stories of The Supernatural Series are books with scary stories that cross the spectrum of Horror, Occult, Ghost, Monster and Fantasy genres.

Stories of The Supernatural Volume 1
SP
Ghosts, demonic creatures, and Death. This collection of Short Stories will haunt and entertain you. Whether it's the classic evil of A Lump of Coal or the whimsy of A Ghost in the House this collection of Short Stories and poems will haunt, thrill and entertain you.
Author: Mark Wilkins **ISBN:** 978-1-936462-18-6 **ASIN:** B01M1N1QR5 **ASIN:** B01MA12YXY (Spanish Edition)

Stories of The Supernatural Volume 2
SP
In this sequel to Stories of The Supernatural there are more Ghosts, Demonic Creatures and Death. This collection of short stories Centers of Ghosts and Monsters. Within its pages you will marvel at the exploits of The Soul Collector, Shudder at the mention of the dreaded Bungadun and of the Hell Banger and ride the rails on the ghost train. Strap on your seat belts, it's going to be a bumpy ride! **Author:** Mark Wilkins **ISBN:** 978-1-936462-26-1
ASIN: B01MDJMSUY **ASIN:** B01M4FXDL1 (Spanish Edition)

A Storyteller Series Continued…
The A Week's Worth of Fiction Series is a series of books with seven stories of fiction each. Each book has stories organized by a particular theme. In a unique twist, each story is followed by a poem which has something indirectly to do with the story that came before it. Readers are asked to read one story and poem that follows it per day. This gives them one day to see how the story resonates with them and try and figure out how the poem is related to the story. To end the suspense, the author includes a section called "How the Poems in this Book are related to the Stories" at the end of the book.

A Week's Worth of Fiction Volume 1
SP

In Volume 1 of A Week's Worth of Fiction, People on The Edge, you will meet people on the edges of society. A security guard who struggles with a dying wife, an elderly man whose cast aside and left to die, one woman struggling to capture romance before her beauty fades and another struggling with cancer. You will meet a little boy who terrorizes a grocery store, a teenage boy searching for love and a small businessman struggling against a monopoly. If you want fictional stories you will never forget you only need to count to 7. **Author:** Mark Wilkins **ISBN: 978-1-936462-13-1** ASIN: B01521SQ02 ASIN: B06XVD21PM **(Spanish Edition)**

A Week's Worth of Fiction Volume 2
SP

Volume 2 of A Week's Worth of Fiction, Science Fiction you will be intrigued and astounded by stories about a girl who has the cure for a deadly disease, a woman on a date with psycho somatic disease called prophecy, a robot chicken, a supernatural fly, an astral projection, a teacher in a new job where everything is not what it seems and a futuristic world where the only economy is barter. If you want science fiction stories you will never forget you only need to count to 7. **Author:** Mark Wilkins
ISBN: 978-1-936462-14-8 **ASIN:** B01LX9RZH7
ASIN: B071GCYFK6 **(Spanish Edition)**

A Week's Worth of Fiction Volume 3
SP

A Week's Worth of Fiction Volume 3, The Many Sides of Violence, features 7 fictional stories that explore violence. One story looks at what goes through the mind of a terrorist about to blow himself up. Another, looks at an executive considering suicide. The plots of other stories include a, man trying to outwit an armed carjacker, a sky marshal trying to figure out which passage is a terrorist, a soldier who realizes someone in his platoon is a serial killer, an ex-convict who has to decide if he should use violence to combat evil and an everyman who becomes a hero through unspeakable violence, if you want violent stories you will never forget you only need to count to 7.**Author:** Mark Wilkins
ASIN: B071WNC6ZX   **ASIN:** B072K6J9HN
(Spanish Edition)

A Week's Worth of Fiction Volume 4
SP

In A Week's Worth of Fiction 4, Realizations, you will meet people from various backgrounds who come to important realizations. You will meet a Doctor who comes to a realization about old age, a politician who struggles to be his own man, a rich man who reaches an epiphany after a chance encounter at a store, A farmer in need of help, A little boy who struggles with a new cell phone that seems processed, a swimmer who gains insight from her morning routine and a police officer who develops empathy for a hardcore gangster. If you want the fictional stories you will never forget you only need to count to 7. **Author:** Mark Wilkins **ASIN: B07217QL6H   ASIN: B071JVQQ96   (Spanish Edition)**

A Storyteller series continued…

The Classroom Confessions Series is a series of books with stories from the front line of public education. Stories and song lyrics mostly focus on students and teachers. Some will make you laugh, others will make you cry but they will all give you insights into public education and entertain you while giving you something to think about.

Classroom Confessions Volume 1
        SP
is a series of true stories from the front lines of public education. Within its pages you will meet quirky characters, the good, the bad and the over caffeinated. Some of them are teachers, some students and some are administrators. Some will make you laugh, others will make you cry but they all play an important role in public education. Their stories are written in way that will entertain you and give you something to think about.
Author: Mark Wilkins **ISBN: 978-1-936462-08-7**
ASIN: B00VNFJBX8   ASIN: B01MSV4N92
(Spanish Edition)

Classroom Confessions Volume 2
                SP

Is another series of true stories from the front lines of public education. Within its pages you will meet unforgettable characters like the French Substitute, Mr. Happyhands, Harry Winkwater, The Bushwhacker and of course, Julian. Some will touch your heart, others will give you something to think about but they will all entertain you. **Author:** Mark Wilkins **ASIN:** B01N1OCRVC
ASIN: B06XC9HDQV (Spanish Edition)

The Love Force Novella Series: These are short novels of varying length.

Karma   **Ppr   SP**

The story of one man who negotiates between two different cultures, and opposing life views competing for his attention. His conflicts and struggles are overshadowed by cosmic forces he cannot understand. Karma provides insights into the struggles and conflicts we all face.
Author: Mark Wilkins

ASIN: B0722R448R   (English Edition)
ASIN: B072Z6L36 (Spanish Edition)

The Beyond Faith Series

Is a series of books that look at life from a spiritual perspective. No matter what your faith, you will find spiritual insights in these books that will enrich your life.

What Faith Has Taught Me
SP

I am just an ordinary person who has been privileged to have a life filled with miracles and revelations. There are many times when I had nothing except faith but faith was all I needed to sustain me. My faith and my God have taught me many life lessons. This book shares some of the things my faith has taught me and the spiritual insights I have gained because of my faith. **Author:** The Prophet of Life **ISBN: 978-1-936462-03-2   ASIN: B01527IKT8 ASIN: B01EE3QSW2   (Spanish Edition)**

Finding God in A Chaotic World   SP
The world can seem so chaotic these days. Many people long for guidance. Many others want to get closer to God. How do you find God amidst the chaos and confusion? How can you discern God's messages from the multi-media blitz we are each bombarded with every day? Some people are part of an organized religion. Others are spiritual without a particular religion. Some are still searching, All of them trying to find God.

In this book, you will learn that The Lord communicates with how The Lord communicates with you. You will learn about the True Nature of God and realize just how profound God's Love and reach are. You will learn the secret of why God's will always prevails. If you are ready for revelations that may change the way you look at life in general and your life in particular, read this book.
Author: The Prophet of Life **ISBN: 978-1-936462-01-8**
ASIN: B00SLLZAAU
ASIN: B0793KDYX3 (Spanish Edition)

Finding God without Religion   **SP**
People of faith are not exclusive to religion. There are many who are spiritual or agnostic. They don't fit into the doctrine, rituals and congregational community of religion. In this wisdom filled volume, people of faith but without an organized religion can gain insights into life, the afterlife and God without being brow beaten or guilt tripped into conversion. This volume is Book 2 of the Revelations of 2012 Beyond Faith series. Part 1 is entitled Finding God in A Chaotic World.
Author: The Prophet of Life **ISBN: 978-1-936462-10-0**
ASIN: B00XKPD86K   **ASIN: B07F5MTFVQ (Spanish Edition)**

Inspiration For All 1
       SP

Selected Inspirational Writings. Whether you are of faith or just in need of inspiration in your life, this book full of inspirational stories, poems and essays will sustain and strengthen you on your journey. **Authors: The Prophet of Life & Mark Wilkins ASIN: B071ZM17V6 ASIN: B071JW8XXH (Spanish Edition)**

Inspiration for All 2
           SP
This is a book of selected inspirational writings by three different authors. It will not only entertain you but will also stimulate your mind by offering you alternative ways of looking at things and opportunities to gain insights. **Authors**: Mark Wilkins, The Prophet of Life & Dr. Goose. **ASIN: B0736JH6M9**   **ASIN: B072WK9JBH (Spanish Edition)**

Outrageous Humor Series
Books of stories and fake news articles for those with an off-beat sense of humor.

Outrageous Stories   **SP**
This book is filled with offbeat humor articles. All of them are fictitious and many of them completely outrageous. No one is safe from being made fun of be they terrorists, Presidents, Dictators, The Movie and Record Business or couch potatoes. If you are college age or older and have an offbeat, irreverent, sense of humor, this book is for you!
Author: Mark Wilkins **ISBN: 978-1-936462-33-9**
ASIN: B01LY3VZJR
ASIN: B07D1RH9W3 (Spanish Edition)

More Outrageous Stories   **SP**
This book is filled with more offbeat humor articles. All of them are fictitious and many of them completely outrageous. No one is safe from being made fun of be they terrorists, Racists, National Holidays or the medical establishment. If you are college age or older and have an offbeat, irreverent, sense of humor, this book is for you!
Author: Mark Wilkins **ISBN: 978-1-936462-33-9**
ASIN: B074Y8LTTJ

Self Help Series
This consists of books by different authors designed to help people improve their lives.

Become The Person You've Always Wanted to Be SP

This self-help book offers a simple, yet profound method of making positive changes in your life. It includes a link to download exclusive, helpful companion worksheets to help you become the person you have always wanted to be.
Author: Mark Wilkins **ISBN: 978-1-936462-39-1**
ASIN: B01MSYVAB6   ASIN:
 B01MSYVU6R   **(Spanish Edition)**

Life Success Kit   **SP**
Spiritual Thought Leader The Prophet of Life helps you clarify what success really means to you through a series of inspirational life lessons designed to give you new perspectives on achieving success and a blueprint for making changes in the things that are preventing you from becoming a success.
Author: The Prophet of Life **ASIN: B01MZ2TSCP**
      ASIN: B078JZGWDH (Spanish Edition)

The Your Life in Rhyme Poetry Series

Is a series of Poetry books unlike any you have ever read whether it is an exploration of life itself through a thematic chapter on each of the various stages of life as in Reflections in The Mirror of Life, The mixture of thought provoking essays and inspirational poetry of Black in America or the exploration of a single topic as in Romance Returns or Life in Verse. The books in this series will have you rediscovering poetry in a way that will make you wonder why you ever avoided it in the first place.

Reflections in the Mirror of Life

This unique book explores life through its harsh realities, pleasant diversions and positive possibilities. The book looks at modern society, the problems it faces, and the people who are a part of it. In a unique twist that's different from most books of poetry, Reflections is divided into five chapters, each of which explores a different theme woven into the fabric of modern life. The tone for each chapter is set by a free verse poem which is followed by a series of rhyming poems on that theme.

Author: The Prophet of Life **ISBN: 978-1-936462-04-9**
ASIN: B00V2TSAXC

Black in America

is an exploration of racism through essays and poems. It spans from the beginnings of the Civil Rights movement through today. It looks at people who have been lightning rods for race relations in America and has some surprising insights into the people and events that have shaped race relations in America for the past 60 years. This book is a good companion for anyone who wants to gain insight into the Civil Rights movement, race relations and racism itself. **Author:** The Prophet of Life
ISBN: **978-1-936462-09-4   ASIN: B00S05QSXA**

Every Lyric Tells A Story   SP
- A collection of unique song lyrics that tell compelling stories about people, their lives, their hopes and dreams. You can find yourself and people you know in many of them. **Authors:** The Prophet of Life & Mark Wilkins   **ASIN: B01NAFDWZW**
ASIN: B07F5N1Y5G (Spanish Edition)

Romance Lives!
Romance Lives is a very special collection of Romantic Love Poems. The poems are arranged to follow the arc of a romance from its early, puppy love stages through its sweet seductions and the blissful wisdom of mature love. If you are searching for Romance in your love relationship or just want some joyful, insightful romantic reading this book is for you! **Authors: The Prophet of Life & Mark Wilkins ASIN: B07D9WY6V5**
ASIN: B07DP7HX9P (Spanish Edition)

Life in Verse

A collection of poems about life. The poems and song lyrics are about people, their lives, their hopes and dreams. You can find yourself and people you know in many of them. **Author:** The Prophet of Life   **ASIN:**

The Best Quotes quotation series
Is a series of books filled with quotes attributed to the
Prophet of Life whose quotes have been used by charities,
corporations, institutions of Medicine and higher learning.
The book includes a license to use any of the quotes as
long as they are attributed to The Prophet of Life.

The Best Quotes About God   **SP**
This short book is filled with some of the more popular
quotes about God attributed to The Prophet of Life. It is
both thought provoking and inspirational. It is filled with
dozens of quotes about God that one can read and copy for
personal use.   **Author:** The Prophet of Life **ISBN: 978-
1-936462-20-9 ASIN: B018P0M8OC   ASIN:
 B01BJXYHLY (Spanish Edition)**

**The Best Quotes on General Subjects
     SP**
This short book is filled with some of the more popular
quotes on general subjects attributed to The Prophet of
Life. The book includes quotes on topics such as life, love,
happiness, crime and punishment, wellness and includes
many of the humorous quotes attributed to The Prophet of
Life. You will find the wit and wisdom in its pages thought
provoking and inspirational. It is filled with dozens of
quotes about God that one can read and copy for personal
use.

Author: The Prophet of Life   ASIN: B01M58L9LW
ASIN: B01M58L9LW (Spanish Edition)

The Best Spiritual Quotes
SP
This book is filled with some of the more popular quotes on Spiritual Subjects attributed to The Prophet of Life. Included are quotes on faith, mercy, life lessons, humanity and spirituality. You should find them to be profound, thought provoking and inspirational. It is filled with many pages of quotes that one can read and copy for personal use. **Author:** The Prophet of Life
ASIN: **B01MQVA87Q**   ASIN: **B07DP68YSF**
(Spanish Edition)

Children's Storybook Series
All books are by Dr. Goose who writes in both prose and rhyming verse.

Classic Children's Stories You've Likely Never Heard SP
Help develop your child's creative abilities and develop their imagination by reading them stories from this book that has no illustrations. Whether it's a story about Prince trying to find the answer to a question, a spider talking about a savior, a kingdom in trouble or a child trying to save the world you will find yourself wanting to read these children's stories with international flavor again and again. This first book in the series is for smaller children.
Author: Dr. Goose **ISBN:** 978-1-936462-40-7
ASIN: B01NAF8QNU   **ASIN:**
B01MR5PR84   **(Spanish Edition)**

More Classic Children's Stories You've Likely Never Heard   SP
This sequel gives you more unknown classics. The book introduces new characters like a little chicken whose life is similar to a person's and a ballad about a hairy man. There is a story about a prince whose refusal causes an international incident. There is even an updated version of classic children's story everyone knows from different character's points of view. This second book in the series helps tweens and juvenile children creative abilities and develop their imagination as stories from this book that has no illustrations either. **Author:** Dr. Goose **ISBN:** 978-1-936462-41-4

ASIN: B074Y8G4JZ   **ASIN:**
B0755YK6NH   (Spanish Edition)

My First Book of Stupid Little Fables   SP
Whether the greed of mooches and lunch thieves, sadistic
children, or bizarre stories about pets this first installment
in the series of irreverently humorous stories with twisted
endings about the selfish and the greedy delivers. It even
has the stupid little drawings! For Juveniles. **Author:** Dr.
Goose
ISBN: 978-1-936462-44-5   ASIN: B07FFCNCQZ
ASIN: B07FFF13N4 **(Spanish Edition)**

My Second Book of Stupid Little Fables   SP
Whether it's well-meaning but incompetent grandmas,
egotistical women, sadistic children, or crazy people in
shopping centers, this second installment in the series of
irreverently humorous stories with twisted endings about
the selfish and the greedy delivers. It even has the
drawings you love to make fun of just like the first one!
For Juveniles. **Author:** Dr. Goose   **ISBN:**
ASIN: **ASIN:**   (Spanish
Edition)

More Children's Stories
School Kidz Volume 1 Elementary and Middle School
SP
Six funny stories about kids who are smarter than their
age. Within its pages you will meet A boy whose
vocabulary is better than the adults in his school, a kid who
escapes a spanking, A kid who gets a new cell phone with
a built in problem and a brother and sister who learn how
get rid of junk from an old aunt. Recommended for kidz
ages 12-16. **Author:** Mark Wilkins **ASIN:** B0717B6SQ4

ASIN: B078JMR7ZB (Spanish Edition)

School Kidz Volume 2 High School   **SP**
9 stories about kids who are in high school. Within its pages you will meet a group of Kidz who get involved in a rotten egg war, a girl who doesn't exist, and a kid who sends a friend on a date with his sister. Recommended for kidz ages 14-18. **Author:** Mark Wilkins **ASIN: B071W5WZZN**

Coming Soon E Workbooks and an E Textbook!

A series of mini and one comprehensive E Textbook Under the title of Mr. Wilkins Teaches English by Mark Wilkins

The specific mini textbooks will be on topics such as Reading and Responding to Literature, and Methods for Writing Paragraphs and Essays. The Comprehensive text will include a weekly spelling component and both the mini texts and comprehensive Text will include creative lessons that promote creativity and critical thinking in students while fitting into common core standards. The mini texts will be no more than 99 cents each and the comprehensive text will be paperback for under $10!
 All of the books are freshly created and contain exclusive intellectual property you won't find in any other texts. These books are perfect for students learning high school English levels 9 & 10 whether you are a classroom teacher or are home schooling your child. We are making the commitment to keep all of the books at low prices to allow parents and school districts to afford texts in the face of shrinking educational budgets. Purchasers will be given an opportunity to receive an email with a printable version of the exercises and assignments as well as links to online testing free of charge.
Author: Mark Wilkins   **ISBN:**   **ASIN:**

Compelling Stories for Adaptation to Short Film
For Film Students

Compelling stories in a set location with six or less characters. Easily adaptable to screenplay with notes on adapting them.
Author: Mark Wilkins   **ISBN:**   **ASIN:**

Loveforce Paperbacks

All of our paperback books cost between $6.50 and $7.50.

Stories of The Supernatural: A Storyteller Series Book SP Loveforce Duo

This collection of 15 stories is filled with ghosts, demonic creatures, monsters and death. It will haunt you, thrill you and entertain you. Within its pages you will marvel at the exploits of The Soul Collector and the uniqueness of Life Lines and Cannibal Money. You will shudder at the mention of a lump of coal or the dreaded Bungadun of Blood Valley and ride the rails on the ghost train. Strap on your seat belts, it's going to be a bumpy ride! **Author:** Mark Wilkins

ISBN-13: 978-1936462537   ISBN-13: 978-1936462575 SP

Karma   SP

Karma is the story of one man who negotiates between two different cultures, and opposing life views competing for his attention. His conflicts and struggles are overshadowed by cosmic forces he cannot understand. Karma provides insights into the struggles and conflicts we all face.

Author: Mark Wilkins   **ISBN-13: 978-1936462506**
ISBN-13: 978-1936462582 SP

A Week's Worth of Fiction Volumes 1 & 2
SP   Loveforce Duo

Whether it's people on the edges of society or Science Fiction Stories, this collection of Volumes 1 & 2 of A Week's Worth of Fiction gives you 2 volumes each with 7 stories that will thrill you, surprise you and make you think. Often dystopic and sometimes surreal, if you want stories you will never forget you only need to count to 7 and you can do it twice in this special paperback edition.

Author: Mark Wilkins ISBN-13: 978-1936462551

Totally Outrageous Stories! Outrageous Satire
Loveforce Trio

There is absolutely nothing that escapes ridicule in this flagrantly outrageous, biting satire of everything you can imagine. This smart, flippant book pokes fun at the entertainment industry, the medical establishment, politics, societal norms, history and science. If you want to laugh to humor with no mercy, you have to get totally outrageous!
Author: Mark Wilkins   **ISBN-10:** 1936462494   **ISBN-13:** 978-1936462490

Slices of Life: Stories of Humor and Pathos (A Storyteller Series)   SP Loveforce Duo

Slices of Life Slices is a collection of humorous short stories about life. Most of them deal with marriage and family members. There are smart spouses, intelligent little children, guys trying to impress their friends and in-laws trying to master technology. Ignorance is the main theme of this book, ignorance that has consequences that are sometimes touching but always humorous. Each story is like a little slice of life but together, they make up an irresistible pie. Sit back, grab a cup of coffee and enjoy some slices of life because, before you know it, you will have finished the whole thing.
Author: Mark Wilkins   **ISBN-13: 978-1936462452 ISBN-13: 978-1936462469 SP**

Public School Confessions: Stories From The Front Lines of Public Education Loveforce Duo SP

Teachers, students and administrators come to life and often clash in dozens of stories from the front lines of public education. Within these pages you will meet people who are smart, rebellious and over caffeinated. Some stories will make you laugh, some will make you cry but they will also entertain you and make you think. **Author:** Mark Wilkins **ISBN-13: 978-1936462056   ISBN-13: 978-1936462063 SP**

The Faith Trilogy   SP   Loveforce Trio

-      This Faith Trilogy Paperback includes three faith filled books: What Faith Has Taught Me, The Best Quotes About God and Inspiration for All: Selected Inspirational Writings. **Author:** Mark Wilkins **ISBN-13: 978-1936462513   ISBN-13: 978-1936462520 (Spanish Edition)**

The Agnostic Faith Trilogy   SP   Loveforce Trio
Three great books combined in one paperback book! You get: Finding God without Religion, The Best Spiritual Quotes and Finding god in a Chaotic World. **Author:** The Prophet of Life
ISBN-13: 978-1936462476   ISBN-13: 978-1936462599 (Spanish Edition)

Black in America
Black in America is an exploration of racism in America through essays and poems. It spans from the beginnings of the civil rights movement through today, It includes powerful new poems "Why We Say Black Lives Matter", "Baltimore", "Requiem for Laquan" It takes a look at people who have been lightning rods for race relations in America and has some surprising insights into the people and events that have shaped race relations in America for thc past 60 years. It is a powerful work that teaches as it entertains and allows the reader gain new insights.
Author: The Prophet of Life
ISBN-13: 978-1936462025

Controversies
    SP

What do Caitlyn Jenner, Donald Trump, Hollywood Sex Scandals, a cure for AIDS, Chinese hackers, Adolf Hitler and Global Warming have in common? They are all at the heart of a controversy and there are stories about them in this unique book that turns tabloid headlines inside out.

Author: Mark Wilkins **ISBN-13: 978-1936462483**

www.ingramcontent.com/pod-product-compliance
Lightning Source LLC
Chambersburg PA
CBHW021927040426
42448CB00008B/943